Burton Harrison

A Daughter of the South

And Shorter Stories

Burton Harrison

A Daughter of the South
And Shorter Stories

ISBN/EAN: 9783744704724

Printed in Europe, USA, Canada, Australia, Japan

Cover: Foto ©Thomas Meinert / pixelio.de

More available books at **www.hansebooks.com**

A

DAUGHTER OF THE SOUTH

AND SHORTER STORIES

BY

MRS. BURTON HARRISON

NEW YORK
THE CENTURY CO.
1899

CONTENTS.

A DAUGHTER OF THE SOUTH.

To look now at the scene of Berthe's fondly remembered childhood would reveal but a melancholy semblance of its old-time stately beauty. The alleys of almond laurel, under which the girl played until the crash of war silenced forever the sweet symphony of her Southern life, are matted and hoary, their arches lost to sight beneath the wedded blooms of wild-growing rose and jasmine. The gardens around the old house are a weedy ruin; the walls of the forsaken dwelling are scarred where patches of stucco have dropped away. But why multiply images of the most distressful fea-

ture of American home history? Everyone
who has journeyed in the South will have
carried away some vision of

> The nakedness and vacancy
> Of the dark, deserted house.

which all the bourgeoning of new prosperity is powerless to efface. Les Amandiers
had been built and named by Berthe's
great-grandfather St. Felix, from whom it
had come by inheritance to her mother,
Mme. de Lagastine.

Early in the century M. Gaston de St.
Felix, then a youngster at his studies in
Paris, had scandalized his friends in New
Orleans by marrying a beautiful girl actress,
whom he transported from the scene of her
early triumphs to a home in the wilderness
across the sea. For her the enamored
young husband had lavished wealth upon
the great stately white house with wings and
galleries and colonnades; for her were the
terraces, with rows of orange and oleander

trees, the flights of steps with vases holding century plants, the gardens with clipped hedges, the fountains, fish ponds, arbors—all fashions of old France designed to comfort the expatriated little Parisienne. At no great distance from one of the most prosperous of the towns built on the lower Mississippi River, in that region pictured as tropical by Chateaubriand in "Atala," but in reality bearing the characteristics of the temperate zone, this earthly paradise had been constructed. But, alas, at a season when the splendid white chalice of the cucumber tree opens its bosom to the sun, the little French lady had put forth her first blossom and faded from the scene.

Berthe's mother, a famous heiress, was, on coming into her majority, the only living representative of the St. Felix line. They had married her to Louis de Lagastine, the handsome scion of an impoverished family of Louisiana créoles, and Berthe was, in turn, the sole offspring of that alliance.

Little Miss St. Felix de Lagastine, as her mother took pains to style her, had but to stamp her foot to call to her service a legion of black folk, old and young, who loved her, shadow and substance, better than the world beside. Her frocks and fineries came twice a year from Paris, and her father admired and applauded everything she did.

The dark side of life to Berthe was her mother, a cold, haughty woman, so devoted to church observance that she needed but a few yards of saints' drapery and a nimbus to entitle her to a niche; who, when she was not telling her beads like an image of yellow wax, sat working endless bands of cross-stitch tapestry; who smiled reluctantly, and disapproved of the friendship between Berthe and her papa.

Mme. de Lagastine, heartily ashamed of her actress grandmother, would never countenance Berthe's early passion for counterfeit emotion. One day her lord, coming in booted and spurred from riding, found his wife paler than usual, her lips compressed, listening in the dressing room of one of the great spare chambers. When she bade him look in and be shocked, he saw through the door's crack a baby star, ranting and raving the speeches of some turbid tragedy of a Restoration dramatist, taken at hazard from the library shelves, all unconscious of the meaning of her eloquence, her cheeks crimsoned, her eyes dilated; around her, on the floor, the rest of the dramatis personæ—small negroes impressed into service, turbaned like Turks, and writhing in death agonies that left an eye open for general observation of occurrences.

"It is the taint in our doomed race," said Mme. de Lagastine drearily.

Berthe, in the act of drinking a conclusive

draught of poison from the *eau sucrée* apparatus on the night-stand by the bed, heard the burst of irreverent laughter her father could not restrain.

" *Allez vous en,* papa," she said vindictively. "You have no right to spy on me. You are dishonorable, and I don't love you one single bit."

Lagastine, persisting, pushed his way into the room, picked up the princess of tragedy, kissed her until she cried out in pain, and swore it was the best fun he ever saw.

"I don't like your choice of a play, little one," he said; "but, by George, you've got the stuff in you that warms the best of 'em."

Berthe saw that she was admired, and immediately the foolish little heart beat high with satisfaction. While at a glimpse of madame's spare figure the dead and dying scrambled away in short order, that lady came into the room, a gleam of sullen anger in her eyes.

"So this is how you second my efforts to bring my child up like a true demoiselle St. Felix?"

"She is all Lagastine, I have heard you say," her husband answered, with a mocking bow. He was a-weary of the St. Felix liturgy. The ten years of it seemed fifty.

"Papa, papa, you dear, sweet, beautiful papa!" Berthe whispered in his ear, as he carried her off to the library to see him lock the cases where the offending dramatists were kept; "I love you, do you hear, I love you. You are my champion, and you make my heart ache with love, sometimes. I will never touch a book on that shelf again whether you lock them up or not."

And Lagastine, with a second glance at her, left the bookcase door as he had found it.

"Mammy Clarisse," announced Berthe to her nurse one night, when the old woman was on her knees taking the shoes and stockings from the little feet she liked to

bare and fondle; "we are going to have a
visitor. To-morrow a boy—a big boy—
named Belmont Carrington is coming to
stay a week. Why, mammy! what makes
you start and cry?"

"My lamb, it's an ole pain," the nurse
said between gasps.

"But there is something—tell me quick,"
said Berthe imperiously.

"It's on'y dat I cawn't hear dat name wid-
out sufferin' agin. Marse Belmont Carrington, de uncle o' dis heah young one dat's
comin', was de master o' my husband, wot
I lost forty years ago."

Berthe felt a remorseful pang. She had
heard the neighborhood's dark story of the
elder Belmont Carrington's departure one
day for New Orleans, where, during a pro-
longed debauch, he had gambled away half
his patrimony and many slaves, including
his body servant, Johnson; she knew that
the offender had committed suicide, and

that Johnson had never come back to the half-crazed Clarisse.

"Oh! how could I forget?" the child cried, leaning over to kiss the wet cheek of her nurse. "Never mind, mammy, I will show this boy that he is not welcome in our house. If papa and mamma want him here, I don't."

"It's no fault o' his'n, honey, wat happened so long ago. But he's got blood in his veins dat will surely bring pain and misery to dem dat loves him. Dey cawn't help deyselves, dem Carrin'tons; dey's beautiful and witchin', but de day comes when you rues knowin' 'em."

Berthe, carrying to sleep with her the wrongs of old Clarisse, awoke determining to keep the new arrival at arm's-length. There was, however, something interesting about a scion of a wicked race through whom misery was sure to come; more interesting than the dapper youths approved by universal voice, who galloped up to the house door on horseback, following the barouches containing visiting parents and unspotted relatives.

So she spent the day in secretly growing impatience for Belmont to arrive, and when the carriage went to meet him at the boat landing began to play Cleopatra with her doll, to while away the time of waiting.

From the verge of the fish pond she launched a barge of gilded osier where, on a bank of real flowers supplying the "strange invisible perfume" that was to "hit the sense of the adjacent wharves," reposed her last and loveliest wax lady from a Paris packing case. Holding a ribbon in his little black paw, a negro boy was instructed to tow the royal barge around the pond, Berthe, with a ragged edition of Dick's Shakespeare, declaiming as she followed. .

Half way, the barge lurched and began to sink. The valiant little darky, wading in to the rescue of her majesty, slipped and was lost to sight. The shrieks of the quarter children brought Clarisse from the arbor where she sat at work, too late to prevent Berthe from plunging to the rescue of Cleopatra's ebon knight.

The families of St. Felix and Lagastine might have lost their representative but for the arrival on the scene of a tall lad of fifteen, who, running down an alley of oleanders, with prompt action fished out of the deepest part of the pond Berthe, clinging to the submerged Cato, who in turn clutched a sovereign well on the way to deliquescence.

To this hero, young Belmont Carrington, a beautiful, manly fellow, whom to see was for most people to love, the little savage princess surrendered heart and brain. She followed him, waited on him, gloried in him; and when, after a week's visit, he went away from Les Amandiers, Berthe cried passionately over her loss and refused

2

to be consoled for many a long day. He had but melted into her dream world of heroes when the war trumpet blew and Les Amandiers passed under the pillar of cloud.

It is one thing to be rich Americans in Paris and quite another to be so limited in means that cab-hire becomes a consideration, and cleaned gloves as much a matter to be aired as one's distinguished antecedents in the States. For some years after the war between North and South the gay French capital appeared to swarm with a succession of families and individuals more or less connected with the recent ravages in the Southern country. Those who were less connected posed heroically as victims of unheard-of cruelty from their conquerors. The enumeration of their losses in flocks and herds, and maid servants and man servants, swelled as the tale went farther. They "took their grievances to walk," as the French saying goes, in every quarter where observation might be counted on. The real sufferers, whom chance or fate had brought into haven there, after the shipwreck of their four years' hope, hugged their sorrows proudly to their breasts. The memory of fire, of famine, of desolated homes, of husbands, sons, and brothers left in soldiers' graves or toiling in exile at any work they could find to put their hands to, was too fresh to bear casual mention.

Among these might be numbered Mme. de Lagastine and her young daughter Berthe, late of Les Amandiers plantation in Mississippi. Berthe, herself, the actual dispenser of finances, was possessor of a bright intrepidity of spirit that made her confront difficulties rather courtingly than otherwise, as offering an agreeable variety of little hills to be skipped over instead of the dead level of a parquet floor to walk on in high-heeled slippers. A girl who, at seventeen, had gone through her experience of conflict and rapine could not class herself with the *jeunes demoiselles* of the society their introductions permitted the dames Lagastine to enter. She often tried to fancy the demure damsels, who had never looked at anything more exciting than the face of a mantel clock or the frown of a mother superior, in one of the many situations of that dark dream of the war. Mme. de Lagastine, hedged in from childhood by prosperity and proprieties, had by now drifted into a chronic state of bewilderment and helplessness. As far as money matters went, Berthe, who had never known where money came from, was a match for her. Their income, sufficient for their wants, was remitted by a banker in New Orleans. For a year or two after their arrival in Paris they had, by the advice of one or two families of old Louisianians settled there, lived in good apartments in a fashionable street. Lessons

began for Berthe. She had certain hours
with a daily governess, others with, respec-
tively—a music master, who came in his
coupé and was always cross and hurried; a
dancing master, who found there was very
little he could teach a young person able to
waltz for hours with scarcely an increase of
the pale glow on her cheek; a drawing master, perpetually harassed by her heretical
ideas on art; and the professors who kept
her hair and finger nails in order at five
francs the séance. Her mother had, of
course, a little carriage in which to take her
drives. Who ever heard of a demoiselle St.
Felix setting foot to earth? And there was
a lady's maid, a man, and a red-cheeked
cuisinière, who ordered everything the
establishment required, while the butler,
when off other duty, skated in baize slippers
over the already shining floors. A modest
establishment in comparison with that of
Les Amandiers, but one that exacted a

comfortable sum to support it; and in the course of time came warning from their man of affairs (an old friend of gallant Colonel de Lagastine, and sincerely anxious to do his best for the widow and orphan) that immediate retrenchment must be made.

Over this letter madame cried a little, observing that it was impossible, barbarous —a fortune like hers to have melted into thin air! asked Berthe to admire the effect of the single-stitch background she was putting into the tapestry intended for the birthday of her gossip Mme. de Tersac; then rang to have hot water renewed in the boule at her feet—and dismissed the subject from her thoughts. Berthe, picking up the offending letter, studied it carefully, an unpleasant belief in its trustworthiness taking possession of her mind. What should she do? Whither turn for counsel? To-morrow, at any rate, she would call on good Mme. de Tersac.

While Berthe's brow was knotting over these problems, and while Mme. de Lagastine stitched, or crooned over the Skye terrier carrying an imperceptible though suspected countenance under an enormous yellow bow, Auguste came into the sitting room with a card upon his tray. ·

"I am engaged. I am always engaged," began madame fretfully; but Berthe pounced upon the card.

"Mamma!" she exclaimed in a whisper, "can you imagine who has found us out? It is someone I knew long, long ago—when I was young—it is Belmont Carrington!"

When, presently, their friend of happier days sat, holding hat and stick, upon an absurdly incompetent gilt chair, they saw how nature had more than fulfilled the promise of his beautiful youth. Oftentimes they had heard of him; knew that, recalled from the university at the beginning of hostilities, he had fought through the war as a member of the famous Washington Artillery; and that, returning after Appomattox to New Orleans, he had found himself to be possessed of a principality in barren acres with which to begin anew the world. Entering the banking house of Mme. de Lagastine's kind agent, Mr. Duval, Belmont had soon been fortunate enough to secure a more lucrative post in Paris. Handsome, well accredited, distinguished for gallantry in service, possessed of unusual charm in manner, he had at once made friends. Berthe had repeatedly heard of him as a bright particular star in the créole colony of Paris, so blent with the old regime of aristocratic France as to be more than a reflection of the Faubourg St. Germain. While he and her mother talked Berthe speculated upon these things, and wondered why his eyes kept wandering around to her with such a curious expression of surprise.

"I had promised myself the pleasure of calling upon you long since, madame," he said, hesitating for a moment as if about rising to take leave. "I will honestly confess that it was one of those visits we defer through accident until we are at last ashamed to show ourselves. To-day I am armed with a letter from my friend, Mr. Duval, who has charged me with a duty I should be glad to put aside. It is about business—he fears that his letters have failed to make you understand—he begs me to explain to you the disposition of certain of your investments."

Madame grew inattentive. She found it impossible to fix her gaze longer upon a subject so uninteresting. At this juncture, with a little toss of the head and a slight inflation of the nostrils, mademoiselle entered the arena.

"I think, if you will, Mr. Carrington, you had better explain to me what Mr. Duval

wishes us to know. It is I who take charge
of my mother's accounts."

"It is no doubt the same old story which
I cannot understand," said the widow wea-
rily.

Belmont looked at Berthe with a new em-
barrassment. From the steady gaze of her
serious eyes he gained courage.

With the papers sent by Mr. Duval open
between them at a little table, they went
over many details hitherto unknown to the
young girl. When the examination was at
an end she pondered briefly, then spoke
composedly:

"We have no right, then, to be living as
we are. The sum you say we may spend
would not pay a fourth part of what we do
spend. To-morrow, Mr. Carrington, I shall
see Mme. de Tersac, who will advise me
where to go."

"It is needless to say you may command
me in any and every way," he answered,

astonished at her composed acceptance of a lot of poverty.

"That we shall, never fear," Berthe said smiling; "I have the most vivid remembrance of the time when you played *Percinet* to my *Graciosa* at the fish pond."

"Oh, I remember now," he cried. "I shall have to own that, until I met you again, I had almost forgotten my rescue of— let me see—what was it, your poodle, your page boy, or——"

"It was me," Berthe interjected loftily.

Decidedly, she regretted her cordiality with this oblivious personage. But when, laughing and apologizing, he took his leave, it seemed to her somehow that sunshine had gone with him. With a sigh, she sat down beside her mother and gently made clear to her the inevitableness of a change in their style of living.

Next day, and often thereafter, Belmont placed himself at the disposal of his countrywomen, to aid in recasting their plans in the narrower mold of cheap lodgings with "table understood." Old Mme. de Tersac, as practical, luckily, as she was kind, herself a New Orleans woman living on nothing in particular a year, took this matter into her own hands, driving about in a fiacre, accompanied by Berthe, and occasionally by Belmont, to find a suitable pension. After several Chesterfieldian spats about terms and privileges with landladies, silvervoiced and rapacious, of each of whom in turn Mme. de Tersac, on returning to the carriage, would aver "that woman is an infamous plunderer, who would sell the bones of her grandmother for cash," the order was given to drive along the Avenue de la Grande Armée, thence beyond the barrier to a villa boarding house, adjoining one of the chief gates of the Bois.

"I left this for the last, my dear, because your poor mamma will have to pay extra cab-hire for the privilege of driving one square beyond the city limits."

"But it is charming!" cried the girl.

"Charming! Perhaps," said the old lady with reserve; "but undoubtedly bourgeois; and I'm wondering how we can ever bring your poor mamma to think of it! A demoiselle St. Felix! But there, there, let's look first and talk afterward. The gate with gilt railings to the left, *cocher;* and I hope this creature won't prove a shark."

It was a bright day of autumn when Berthe exclaimed with pleasure at her first view of Bois Dormant. The inner walls of the house and its dependencies, built around a flagged and shady courtyard into which peeped the treetops of the Bois, were covered with overlapping ivy, save where the jewel brightness of white-curtained windows broke the green façade. In many of these windows bloomed pots of hardy flowers, and the garden beds below were gay with blossoms. A colony of brown birds, chattering ceaselessly, were the only tenants of the yard.

" Pretty, pretty place ! " said Berthe. "Why is it so still?"

"Because the boarders are all old people, my dear, and—— Ah! Mme. la Propriétaire, no doubt!"

Mme. la Propriétaire, in black silk, with a velvet jacket, a tulle cap with pink rose-buds, a gold watch ticking at her waist, a mustache that would have been the glory of a college lad, received *ces dames* with the usual effusion of her class. Yes, there was a *rez-de-chaussée* still to let, with meals at the pension table, where madame, the mother of mademoiselle, could be made most comfortable; a little garden, a *ber-ceau*, oh! a *berceau*—and in spring the nightingales of the Bois—the boarders all excellent people—people settled, people delicate, whose candles are put out by ten o'clock. Mademoiselle herself would, no doubt, arrive from boarding-school, to visit madame her mamma on Sundays?

Belmont laughed at Berthe's majesty of mien, and Mme. de Tersac hastened to explain that her friends were the widow and daughter of a Confederate officer, killed in the late war in America, who required accommodations together, as well as quarters for their maid.

Mme. la Propriétaire's brow puckered with instant sympathy. Truly, the *rez-de-chaussée*, with the garden and the *berceau*, seemed designed by Providence for the retreat of *ces dames;* she had heard of that sad war in l'Amérique du Sud, but pardon, was not mademoiselle a trifle fair for one of her oppressed race? One of the boarders— a sister of the lamented genius Baras, the great romancer—was also a mulatto, but darker far in tint than mademoiselle!

The ringing silver of Berthe's laugh refused to be restrained. It rippled into the still precincts of Bois Dormant, and set the birds to chirping more busily than before.

His friends established in their new abode, Belmont's commission from Mr. Duval was at an end. But many a time, out of the busy, brilliant world of Paris, his feet turned aside to seek the quiet spot where, in a little salon hung with thread-bare crimson stuff, Mme. de Lagastine sat in her easy-chair working eternal tapestries, and Berthe hovered, fresh, sparkling, full of infinite variety, welcoming him with all her ingenuous soul within her eyes. To her he was not only the boy champion illumined with the light of Les Amandiers, the ideal soldier of the Lost Cause, but a comrade in whose society her youth had begun to bloom again, her sad memories to fade. Often they walked together in the Bois, in company with Berthe's neighbor from the attic floor above, Mme. Letellier, a gentle old woman who had conceived a strong friendship for the solitary girl. Sometimes Berthe and he dined with Mme. de Tersac, to go to opera or theater. Once Carrington was allowed to entertain the girl and her kind old friend with a dinner followed by the play. But her mother's declining health and their narrow circumstances shut Berthe out, in general, from the pleasures of her age. Carrington felt that in her he had discovered a virgin island rich in budding fruit and bloom, the right to which there was none to dispute with him. His easy success in bringing light to her eyes, and pink to her clear pale cheeks, intoxicated him. All the while he was stung by an inward conviction that a knowledge of his real self, his life, would, if known to her, cause Berthe pain beyond all imagining. Each day he resolved to explain to her his actual position, to make clear certain restraining circumstances that

3

held him bound; and each day Berthe's sweet presence witched him to self-indulgence.

One bright winter's day, through the kind offices of Mme. de Tersac's friend, the Duc de Bassano, came rose-colored tickets of invitation to a ball to be given at the Tuileries in honor of certain "visiting sovereigns." It was all very well, Berthe thought joyfully, for some of her mother's friends, who were moldy old Legitimists, to sigh and shake their heads over the idea of their accepting. Mme. de Tersac, immolating herself in an old blue velvet, with ofttimes cleaned point de Venise, that had seen many a court festivity, had secured the services as escort of the Comte de Barrot, who, though no lover of the present court, came sometimes across the Seine to look in upon its extravagances; and with such a background of respectability even Mme. de Lagastine could not find fault.

Who shall sing of the glories of our heroine's first ball? From the moment when, rumpling herself into the corner of the brougham in order not to crush her young lady's tulle, Mme. de Tersac called out in her hoarse old voice, "To the Tuileries, Adolphe," Berthe's spirit was on wings.

At the foot of the grand staircase of fifty steps, carpeted with crimson and lined on either side by the splendid phalanx of the emperor's Cent Gardes, between whose ranks flowed a glittering stream of men in court costume, with swords and orders, and women borne down under the weight of hereditary gems, they were met by the count, a stately *vieux moustache* with snow-white hair, whose eye kindled approvingly at sight of his youthful charge.

When, in the radiance of myriad wax lights, caressed by the strains of Strauss waltzes led by Strauss, they paused in the

great Salle de la Paix for breath, hustled on
every side by a dazzling, pushing, courteous
multitude, Berthe's wonder found vent in
words.

"You must try to fancy it," said the
count, "as I saw this room when the palace
was held by the mob in Forty-eight. I
suppose a young lady would shudder at the
idea of the National Guards bivouacking
here on trusses of hay, eating their bread and
sausage and drinking the wine their majesties had left behind; but to me it was very
picturesque."

"I am not that kind of a young lady,"
Berthe answered. "Our own dining room
at Les Amandiers, in Mississippi, was so
used by the soldiers during one of the Fed-
eral raids. We women kept ourselves
locked in upstairs with loaded pistols, which
we fortunately did not need. I shall never
forget that long night spent in listening to
their songs and shouts. When they left us

next day, it was as if the Egyptian locusts
had passed over the place"

"I had forgotten that it is a true daughter of Mars whom I have the honor to
escort," said the count. "Now, mesdames,
if you please, we had better push on to the
Salle des Maréchaux. Ah! what a crowd!
It will need a stronger arm than mine to
open a way for both of you."

"Can I be of service, Count?" asked a
gentleman, against whom they were thrown
by a buffet of the throng.

"Ah! Meester Ludlow, you are very
good. Permit me to introduce you to
Mme. de Tersac and to your charming
compatriot, Mees de Lagastine. If you will
give your arm to mademoiselle. There.
En avant! March!"

Berthe saw the valiant count and breathless little Mme. de Tersac borne away
from her without resistance. A rumor that
their Majesties had come in swayed the

entire mass of people in the direction of the
Salle des Maréchaux, blazing with gilded
fretwork just ahead.   Giving a side glance
at her companion, she discerned that he was
tall, blond, and stalwart, carrying himself
with a military air that became him well.
In turn, his rather cold blue eyes were scan-
ning her with an expression she could not
but resent.

"You did not expect to be burdened with
a girl?" she said, with a childish impulse to
withdraw her arm from his.

"We will discuss that when I have succeeded in restoring you to your friends," he
answered indifferently, and then the current
swept them on.   In vain the *chambellans*
shouted " R-r-éculez-vous, messieurs et
dames, s'il vous plait"; the throng moved
forward as one man.   It was a crush in
which the fairest arms were excoriated by
contact with neighboring epaulets; where
swordhilts were pressed into adjacent ribs;

where a fat lady, requesting a gentleman to be good enough to remove his finger from her ear, was answered politely that nothing would give him greater pleasure were not the thing physically impossible just then!

When, at length, brought up against a gilded railing, Berthe found herself in a wreck of tattered tulle, it was at the moment when Louis Napoleon and Eugénie—she fair as a swan, radiant and gracious, aglitter with a thousand gems—accompanied by their royal guests, were in the act of seating themselves upon their golden chairs of state. Around them upon the dais was grouped such a constellation of dignitaries as made it appear that all Europe and the Orient were focussed upon the left bank of the Seine. Berthe, forgetting all besides, bloomed with excitement, rained questions, devoured Ludlow's information, and ended by charming him with her *naïveté*.

"You can say you have seen the Second

Empire at flood tide of glory, certainly," he said, at the end of half an hour.

"But I am awfully disappointed in its chief," she cried. "He is little and yellow, and looks half asleep. Most of the grandees, in fact, are disappointing; but their clothes and jewels are all I could desire. Thank you so much for enlightening my ignorance. I am only afraid I've bored you."

"Promise to let me settle that score with you at another time," he began, with a smile that reassured her, when an amused voice at Berthe's elbow made her start.

"Here you are, in the front rank of stargazers," said Carrington. "If you knew at what peril to life and limb I crossed to you! Colonel Ludlow, I am commissioned by Mme. de Tersac to restore to her your charge."

As Ludlow bowed and moved away, Berthe laid her hand on Carrington's arm and whispered eagerly, "Who is Colonel Ludlow? He has been so very kind to me."

"Ludlow?" said Belmont carelessly, "why, one of our conquerors. The best fellow in the world."

" A *Yankee* officer?"

"Certainly, and a distinguished one. We had, when we first met in Paris, been figuratively engaged in popping bullets at each other during the four years past, but are now on amicable terms."

"Oh! how can you jest?" she said in her tragic way. "You who have fought through all—you who upheld our glorious banner till it trailed in dust. I understand now why I disliked him at first sight."

Fire flashed from her eyes. Belmont, to hide a smile, turned and looked at a far window-seat shrouded in velvet dotted with golden bees. There, limp and yawning, sat Mme. de Tersac, her lace torn, her poor blue velvet whipped out of shape, her feet aching, but thankful to find a chair. Beside her, erect and gallant, the old count stood beckoning.

"I am glad, mademoiselle, that you were cared for by my excellent friend Ludlow," he said, when the party came again together. "I felt safe in presenting to you a compatriot so well indorsed by your amiable meenester, le Général Deex."

"He is not my amiable minister," exclaimed rebel Berthe pettishly. But she felt, when she caught the twinkle in Belmont's eyes, that she had not aquitted herself with heroic dignity.

On the morning of Christmas Eve Berthe's light feet sped up the stairs, flight after flight, to the attic of Villa Bois Dormant.

"*Entrez*," said a sweet voice, as she knocked at a door under the eaves.

Berthe turned the knob and found herself in a large room with sloping ceilings, the space divided by screens, walls, and windows, hung with glazed chintz scattered with rosebuds and green leaves, floor brightly waxed, a sunny window full of birds and plants. This was the nest of Mme. Letellier, Berthe's chosen friend of all the ancients of Bois Dormant, a swarthy, bright-eyed little lady, who had been a prize pupil of Samson in the Conservatoire and had made a successful *début* at the Odéon many a long year agone. Leaving the stage, temporarily, to marry, she had, upon the birth of her first child, been stricken with a malady that robbed her of strength and voice.

"We lived then in a little cottage at Asnières," the old woman had told Berthe. "Thither came my old associates to condole with me; Louise, from the Comédie Française, Clémentine from the Gaieté. They would bring in at the door a whiff of the air

that intoxicates me even now—the true air
of the theater that the actor does not forget.
They would rustle and chatter and boast
while I would rock the cradle and listen, my
heart tugging at its leash.   Oh, then it was
that I seemed again to hear the great wave
of applause, on which a player rides into his
paradise—I, who had tasted my moment of
success!"

"And what then, dear madame?"

"Eh! what then?   My tempters went
away, my boy awoke and cried for nourish-
ment, my good husband came in from his
work.   We had means enough, we loved.
No, no, there are sorrows in life more
poignant than to renounce ambition.   Mine
were to come.   What was I, after all,
but 'encore une étoile qui file, file et
disparait.' "

"Now I know what an artist you were—
you are!" cried the girl; "to hear you say
that line of Béranger was like the breath of

an Æolian harp. But tell me more about your life."

"After I was a widow and had suffered in many ways, I thought myself lucky to secure this asylum under the roof-tree of a quiet house. When I rented it, *ma foi*, Mme. Thonet was surprised—it had been used as a garret only. I was poor, and little by little have hung the walls with my own hands, have added books, flowers, furniture, as you see. It is a good air that I breathe here, and in spring the treetops of the Bois make a green murmuring ocean beneath me as I sit at the window sewing."

"And your son, madame? Does he come on Sundays with his wife and little ones to take you home to dinner, like the rest?"

"No, my child," the old Frenchwoman said gently. "When the emperor sent Maximilian into Mexico my boy went too. See, there is all that is left me of my son."

And Berthe's eyes, following the indica-
tion of her finger, saw on the wall a soldier's
picture swathed in crape; above it the tri-
color of France.

"Ours is a common grief, madame. My
father also lies in a soldier's grave," she
answered, bursting into the old hot tears
that had seemed in Confederate days to
come from a bottomless fountain. It was
madame, dry-eyed and tender, who soothed
her into repose.

After that time Berthe's intimacy with
the old woman had rapidly increased. Madame lent her books—first, grudgingly, as
to a *jeune fille* of France—"La Colombe"
of Alexander Dumas, pure as its title, "La
Tulipe Noire," and "La Mare au Diable,"
the lovely idyl of George Sand; afterward,
with astonishment at her maturity of taste,
dramatists, ancient and modern, from whose
pages Berthe was bidden to read and recite.
In return, Berthe saved for her fruit and

bonbons, welcomed as a canary welcomes sugar in his cage; and the girl's pretty fashion of stealing in with violets for the hanging cup beneath the soldier's portrait on the wall sealed to hers indissolubly the old woman's loving heart.

To-day Berthe was in high spirits. Carrington had written to propose to Mme. Letellier and herself to attend with him the midnight mass at the Madeleine. To please her, to waken that bright look of girlish joy in her face, Belmont was even prepared to run away from a dinner of men to which he was engaged, and sit half the night on a hard chair in the surge of a crowd combining sensationalism with enforced religious observance.

Berthe found her friend in street costume, her face pale, her eyes red with weeping.

" *Tenez, mon enfant,* it is the anniversary of my greatest sorrow," the old woman said. "Since early this morning I have been in

the Chapelle Expiatoire to pray for my lost
Élise."

"A daughter, too? All you loved dead?
Poor, poor madame!"

A look of anguish came into the mother's
face.

"She is not dead. It would have been
better had she died. It is a whole year
since she left me," she cried chokingly.

Berthe started, shuddering. For the life
of her she could not govern the chill that
held her in its grip. The stricken mother,
offering no protest, simply bent her head
forward and stood waiting. Then blushing
hotly, and with a keen impulse of remorse,
Berthe exclaimed "Oh! I was cruel to let
you see my heart."

"Not so, my child. It is part of my
cross that I must daily and nightly bear,"
the widow answered gently. "But, oh! to
lie down and to rise up knowing that this
great city holds hidden one so dear, one that

no hand of mine may rescue. Ah me! God's
will be done. My *petite* Berthe will forgive
me that I had not courage to tell her this
before. She will forget the poor sinner who
is part of me; she will not withhold from
me her love?"

"Trust me," said Berthe.

Since ten o'clock they had been seated in
the nave of the vast church, in a semi-dark-
ness that hid the tracery of carved stone,
the mosaic of many-colored marbles, the
luster of gilded chapels. Around them the
crowd gathered to the utmost limits of the
interior—a strange, mixed company of dev-
otees, from the *boulevardier fini* in evening
clothes reeking with fumes of cigars and
wine, kneeling side by side with the peasant
woman in her turret cap, to the *petite dame*
in sables, telling her beads with downcast
eyes at the elbow of some workman, swart
and grimy spite of his new-washed blouse of

4

blue. Through the night these people were to troop up continually to the high altar, scattering, after the most solemn communion of the year, to resume their several avocations. Berthe, heedless of incongruities, rapt in a trance of pleasure, sat with Belmont beside the old madame, who for the most part knelt, lost in devotion, upon the marble flags. At no time had the girl felt so near, so deliciously at rest with him to whom she had now come to surrender the love of her maiden heart. They spoke rarely, to exchange whispers in which each strove to repress the trembling of happy voices fraught with tenderness.

To Berthe it was as if they two had secured some little island around which an ocean surged to cut them off from humanity less blest. To Belmont, alas! this was but a time of indulgence too precious to be given up, too perilous to be repeated.

Then, from behind the sculptured angels

of the high altar issued a blast as of silver trumpets, and over the kneeling multitude burst a flood of light. During the pageant of the mass a man's voice chanted Adolphe Adam's "Noël":

"Minuit, Chrétien !   C'est l'heure solennelle
Où l'Homme-Dieu descendit sur la terre."

Berthe sat spellbound until the triumphing refrain:

"Noël! Noël! Voici le Rédempteur!"

swelled to the full force of a glorious barytone, and the organ caught up and swept away the strain.

"I feel as if I had touched the gate of heaven," she whispered to Carrington, who smiled and answered that the famous singer from the opera house was in very good form to-night, certainly. Belmont did not care how long this sort of thing went on, so that he might watch the girl's face glowing and paling like an aurora borealis.

Suddenly she looked at a point near one of the chapels at the side.

"Anyone you know?" he asked carelessly.

"The strangest thing," she said; "I felt as if someone were impelling me to look, and, over there, I saw such a sad white face gazing at us—a girl, beautifully dressed, with golden hair; there, do you see? no, she has vanished in the crowd."

"I saw her—rather an unusual type of her class—a little 'off,' probably. Please, when you have any glances to bestow, turn them this way."

"Hush!" said Berthe reprovingly. During the remainder of the service she could feel nothing but the fullness of content. As they came out into the struggling dawn of Christmas morning, through the vestibule that was a few years later to be the scene of the Communist slaughter by the troops, she saw Colonel Ludlow with a party of Americans. To her present exalted state of mind he was an interruption, a cloud. While bestowing on him a frosty little nod, she wondered at a certain indefinable shadow in his eyes, which, from a person privileged to bestow on her compassion, might have been interpreted into expressing that emotion.

Carrington put the ladies into a fiacre to set off on their long drive to Bois Dormant. Standing upon the sidewalk, hat in hand, the familiar brilliant smile upon his face, Berthe's last glimpse of him filled her heart with a proud joy.

To have seen the society of Villa Bois Dormant at its best—before the siege of the Versailles troops in 1871 laid low the quaint old domicile and worked havoc in the bowery streets surrounding it—one should have waited until evening brought out the antique butterflies in what they called their "toilets for the day." At the *déjeuner de midi* the groups around the tables in the great bare dining room resembled a collection of shrunken chrysalids. Equipped in skull caps, camisoles, curl papers, snuffy coats, or dingy short gowns — generally omitting wigs and teeth—the old creatures mumbled and grumbled, compared symptoms, mixed doses, scolded Mme. la Propriétaire and her minions, and often went through the ceremony of threatening to change their quarters to the pension across the way.

It was at dinner, when the lamps were lighted and some vases of artificial flowers lent to the tables a festal air, that the old ladies emerged in gayest attire of silk and velvet, with tiers of snowy curls or frontlets of jetty black; the men, shaven and spruce, in tight-fitting black coats showing the inevitable red button of honor on the breast; all chattering, laughing, bandying jests and compliments, offering snuffboxes, and waving handkerchiefs of flaring silk.

Christmas week having passed without

especial celebration, the dawn of New
Year's day woke up, in common with all
Paris, the Villa Bois Dormant. Directly
after the first breakfast, set in a procession
of servants and tradespeople, even including
the merry little Auvergnat cobbler who had
once mended a rip in Mlle. Berthe's shoe, to
offer compliments and smiles and to receive
reward according to the limit of the giver's
purse. Then the boarders, attired as for
Sunday junketings abroad, came fluttering
out into the sunshine of the green-walled
court. The air was full of shrill pipings of
good-fellowship. Next, flinging wide the
gilded gates of the *porte-cochère*, Belgian
Antoine stood, with his crumpled face relaxed into a broad smile of welcome. In
trooped a gay medley of married sons and
daughters, leading or carrying their little
ones, each laden with a New Year's offering
of flowers or sweets. To find out *bon papa*,
to surprise *bonne maman*, was the order of

the hour. Nothing was heard but outcries
of pleasure and caressing. Bearded men
kissed each other on both cheeks, kissed the
grandparents, kissed the children; when the
tumult subsided there arose the quavering
exclamations of the old people upon the
schoolboy's growth and uniform, the baby's
teeth, the young matron's bravery of lace
and jet and fur. A ceremony not omitted
was the formal presentation to fellow boarders of families known, through the daily
gossip of Bois Dormant, from A to Z. And
at last, after a visit to the quarters of *bon
papa* or *bonne maman* in search of *étrennes*
hidden there, the merry crowd dispersed.
Bonneted, cloaked, cosseted by their young,
the boarders were carried off in triumph to
finish the day *en fête.*

Well pleased to be sought by Berthe,
Mme. Letellier that afternoon quitted her
solitude beneath the eaves to walk with the
young girl along the boulevards, where the

whole bright world of Paris seemed to have flung itself upon the street in a delirium of fun. In Berthe the Southern gayety of nature, ever quick to be aroused, made instant answer to the challenge of this brilliant atmosphere touched but not chilled by frost, the booths edging for miles the sidewalks, the ambulating venders—of hot drinks carried in reservoirs upon their backs, of flowers, of "gauffres et plaisirs, M'sieurs et Mesdames"—the black throngs of sightseers, the bands of maskers, the incessant ripple of merriment tinkling along the lines. Herself an unconscious picture in the toque and fur-bordered pelisse of Polish cut, all russet-brown in tint save for the red rose nestling at her breast and the clear shining of her happy face, she walked with a free, quick stride with which madame's mouse-like steps had much ado to keep company.

Madame, shrewd and anxious, had a fair

suspicion of the origin of some part of Berthe's exhilaration on this *Jour de l'An.* That morning had arrived, with a card from Carrington, whom she had failed to see since the night of the midnight mass, a basket of gilded osier overflowing with red roses and white lilacs; after it, a box sent by express from Nice from the gardens of the poet florist, Alphonse Karr, in which, bedded in large and luscious violets, lay a tangle of wet jasmine that might have twined on the galleries of Les Amandiers.

"Who could have divined my longing to smell jasmine again?" Berthe had wondered, laying the sprays against her cheek, drinking in the familiar fragrance, shutting her eyes to dream of her ruined home.

"Mamma, madame, see here!" she had cried eagerly to her two observers. "Not a note or a card to say who has made my New Year dawn so happily."

"Some one of our Southern friends, no doubt," said Mme. de Lagastine, looking up for a moment with lackluster eyes. "One, two, three greens and one red. You grow more like your father, child. Will you remember to tell the person of the house that I cannot put up with the draught from that window another day."

Although Berthe wore loyally one of Belmont's roses, "the scent of that jasmine flower" followed her throughout the wintry walk. It was, therefore, with not only surprise but distaste that she found herself accosted in the thickest of the throng by the man of all others least in touch with her happy reverie. Ludlow, who could not well have failed to read her impulse in her artless face, wasted no time in idle ceremony.

"You will pardon me, I hope," he said in French to include madame, "but I don't think you ladies should walk along this square alone. There is a party of masqueraders just ahead who are likely to get into mischief with the police if they keep on their present line. If you don't mind, I shall go with you until you have passed the spot."

"Thank you," said Berthe briefly, while madame poured out more bounteous courtesies. To recede was worse than to go on. Ludlow, keeping close ahead of Berthe, madame following, used his shoulder as a wedge to open a way through the multitude now unpleasantly astir. For it needs but such a trifle to shift the temper of a Paris crowd from gayety to anger. A bourgeois, insufficiently excusing himself for treading on his neighbor's toe in his zeal to push forward to see he knows not what, may in an instant transform these smiling revelers to a semblance of the human tigers of the past tragedies of Paris streets. Startled by the ominous mutter of the excited throng, Berthe instinctively glanced at the house-

front nearest them, hoping to find a refuge.
On the balcony above, a party of people in
street dress had come out to look at the
panorama of the boulevard. Behind the
others, leaning down with the bright look of
interest Berthe knew so well, was Belmont
Carrington in close conversation with a
woman.

"Handsome, well bred, well dressed, not
too young," was Berthe's mental inventory.
"How many friends he has we do not know!
I am glad he does not see me hustled in
this crowd. I will not look again because—
well, because I want to look." At this
point of her speculation she lost count of
minor incidents. The police, interposing,
had forced a vent ahead for the passage of
the strugglers. A portion of the crowd surrounding the drunken maskers was pushed
between the booths into the street. A
scream in a woman's voice was followed by
oaths, shouts, the trampling of horses, a

fresh rush of the crowd. Berthe, carried
resistlessly toward the point of excitement,
found herself, to her dismay, caught up in
Ludlow's arms, and, to avoid being violently
hurled upon the asphalt, held for a long moment clasped to his breast. The words of
reluctant gratitude tempered with shame-
faced rebuke that, when she was set in
safety down, rushed to her lips were silenced
by the stern reality confronting her. Almost at her feet lay a young lad, pale and
lifeless, his short golden hair brushing the
knee of the gendarme who had dragged him
from beneath the hoofs of a pair of spirited
horses attached to a brougham, in which sat
two gentlemen on their way to make calls of
the *Jour de l'An*, laden with costly flowers
and *bonbonnières*. Upon her first glance at
the still face, shadowed by sunny locks from
which the cap had fallen away, Berthe, with
a thrill, recognized the features of the girl
whose mournful gaze she had encountered

at the Madeleine. The puzzle was made clear when, uttering a strange cry that pierced the bystanders' hearts with sympathy, Mme. Letellier ran forward and fell upon her knees beside the inanimate figure, calling out, "Élise, *ma fille*, Élise!"

"It is her daughter, who has been lost," Berthe whispered tremblingly in Ludlow's ear. "Oh, what shall we do?"

"A little actress of the Bouffes, no doubt, who is masquerading in boy's clothes," said a bystander.

"*Mais non*, my little cabbage, she is not dead," panted a fat bourgeoise, whose husband had elbowed for her a way to the front ranks of lookers-on. "*Tiens*, Joseph, she breathes. Madame her mother will have difficulty to remove her from this crowd."

In the confusion of the scene Berthe felt rather than saw that Ludlow's chief concern was to withdraw her from contact and iden tification with the centers of interest.

"You treat me like a child," she exclaimed. "What can it matter beside her
trouble? Oh, I must go to poor madame!"

"Madame would be the last person to
desire your presence now," he said peremp-
torily urging her back into the throng upon
the sidewalk.

"I have never been dictated to before; I
have been many times able to help in emer-
gencies; I cannot leave my poor old friend
in such a dreadful strait," she protested,
fairly vexed.

"It is impossible that you should mix
with this affair," he returned briefly. "If
you will remain here in the doorway beside
some of the family folk who have taken
refuge from the crowd, I shall go and do all
that can be done."

Conquered, though far from convinced,
by the quiet decision of his manner, Berthe
obeyed with the best grace at her command.
Her heart swelled with pity for her friend

and her conscience accused her of cowardice in holding back from active service in the poor woman's behalf. Waiting impatiently, she at length saw Ludlow pushing toward her through the crowd.

"There has been a delay," he explained. "The men whose horses ran her down were at first inclined to do everything necessary in the case, but the testimony of bystanders and of the gendarme who witnessed it unites in saying that the wretched creature threw herself deliberately in the way of the approaching carriage. The police had just warned her to behave with more discretion, when she broke away from the officer whose hand was on her shoulder, and it was over in a flash. Under these circumstances the owners of the horses decline to interfere, and the case must be left to take the usual course."

"Will she die?" asked Berthe.

"That cannot be known until they get her

5

to the hospital. The poor mother, who is quite composed, thinks of everything, and has besought me to keep you apart from them, for your mother's sake, she says. Now, if you can rely on me to do what is best for you in this trying emergency, I will see you safely home, and I promise to look out afterward for Mme. Letellier to the extent of my ability."

"But there is something else," she said gratefully. "I am sure madame has little or no money, and if you will please take my purse to her——"

"I have attended to all that," he interrupted. "They are to have every consideration that the authorities will allow."

"Thank you a thousand times," cried Berthe, flashing upon him one of her enthusiastic glances. "If you knew the poor woman's story you would realize how well your kindness is bestowed. And you have given me the only comfort possible in having to turn my back and leave her in such distress."

"You could do nothing whatever except in a sentimental sense," he replied; "and a Paris street crowd on a fête day is hardly the place for the exhibition of a young girl's sympathies. Be sure that Mme. Letellier—whose face carries its own sad story — will be best relieved by having you returned promptly to your mother's care."

By the time he had secured a cab all trace of the episode—a page torn from the daybook of Paris life—had been swept from the street, and, renewed in merriment, the sparkling throng poured up and down the boulevards. Shocked and saddened beyond expression, Berthe was in no mood for making conversation, and the drive along the Champs Élysées and the Avenue de la Grande Armée to Neuilly passed almost in silence. Certainly, to the handsome and distinguished young officer who had put himself about to perform such acts of kindness, the sense of virtue must have been its own reward. Berthe, in one corner of the *fiacre*, her hands clasped in her muff when she was not mopping her eyes from time to time, thought alternately of the mother and child so strangely re-united and of Belmont's attitude toward the pretty, stylish woman with the tired look in her eyes, who had appeared somehow to appropriate his talk. After passing the *bar-rière* she roused from these meditations to a sense of courtesy withheld.

"You will allow me to present you to my mother, Colonel Ludlow?" she said form-ally. "The obligation you have placed us under is so great——"

"That's a small matter," he said, smiling. "But I should like to feel that I have carried out Mme. Letellier's wish literally; and I suppose," he added, hesitating, *"les con-*

venances of a French pension would be better satisfied."

"Oh, I had not thought of that," cried Berthe scornfully. "You cannot imagine what it is for a girl who has grown up in America in war time to be hedged in by all these petty proprieties. But you are right. The Villa Bois Dormant must be propitiated. Luckily the place is almost deserted at this hour, and most of them will be spared the shock of seeing me arrive alone with you. As old Mme. Jérome told me the other day, about my crossing the courtyard with the upholsterer, much is pardoned to an American 'young miss,' brought up to roam unattended in the virgin forests of her *pays sauvage.*"

There was, after all, only the old porter to be scandalized as their cab rolled into the courtyard. Mme. de Lagastine, coming out of her silks and wools to hear Berthe's excited narrative, received Colonel

Ludlow with polite frigidity. To her he was the incarnate type of wrongs and losses that a slight service to her daughter could not put out of sight. Ludlow, lingering for a moment before the grate with its heaped-up billets of wood, an extravagance of the American ladies styled by their fellow lodgers a "*feu d'enfer*," felt an impulse of strong compassion for the child whose sole protector was this cold, impassive creature, so locked in from human sympathies. Promising Berthe to send her early word of the condition of Mme. Letellier's affairs, and receiving a perhaps tardy, but certainly gratifying acknowledgment of her indebtedness to him, in a smile that was like a sunburst, he took his leave.

"I am afraid I am getting to like him," she meditated, while sitting that night in the light of the dying fire, combing her dusky locks. "That is, if I were not a tiny bit afraid of him; and I don't like to be afraid.

Belmont, now, has such a lovely sunny nature one feels like basking in his neighborhood. He draws to him every heart and holds it. Ah me, I had hoped, until just a little while ago, that he would find time to come to us to-day. Perhaps those people were friends just arrived, to whom he was obliged to show civility. I shall tell him, though, how devoted that little *tête-à-tête* behind the rest appeared. She is too old. She looks hard to please, and cynical. Oh, what does it matter? How he will chaff me for my foolishness."

Late in the afternoon she had received from Mme. Letellier a note, penciled in the hospital, informing her of a shade of improvement in the condition of the patient, who was, however, seriously injured and might not survive.

"The *commissionaire* who carries this takes also a line to Mme. Thonet, who will send what I need," the note went on to say.

"Until God wills that her misery shall pass
into His keeping, my place is at her side.
It is thanks to noble M. Ludlow that I and
my poor unfortunate are treated here with
high consideration. When I pray for her
whom the good God has rendered into my
longing arms—for you, tender child, who
have blossomed upon my solitary pathway
to the tomb—must I not also include him,
this stranger who has poured upon me a
bounty so undeserved, so lavish?"

"Poor, dear madame!" thought Berthe,
weaving her veil of hair into plaits that, as
she stood, touched the hem of her trailing
skirts, "hers is a grateful heart. He has
behaved splendidly, if he is a Yankee colonel. Few men would have felt called on to
do so much for perfect strangers. Perhaps
he went into the war so young that he was
not entirely responsible. Maybe he is conscious of wrong done, and is trying to atone
to the South through me. When I think

that he actually held me in his arms, even if it was to save me from being crushed, I feel so angry and ashamed. If he had ever heard half I've said against them, he'd have dropped me quick enough. Belmont will laugh at me, I know."

A tap at the door withdrew Berthe from the incidents of her eventful day to admit Henriette, the cherry-cheeked maid of all work, yawning and holding a letter in her hand.

"It has just arrived, mademoiselle, and the porter is in a temper incredible because he was called after ten o'clock."

"Give it to me. I will make peace with M. Antoine to-morrow," Berthe cried, recognizing upon the envelope the handwriting of Belmont Carrington. When again alone, for a moment she held her treasure, yearning over it, yet begrudging herself the taste of it; then, to make herself amends, tore it open in hot haste and read its contents with a fast throbbing heart.

"To-night, by the midnight train," wrote Belmont, "I start for London, to be absent some two weeks on business for the firm. I am writing this lest you should wonder why I have not in person offered you such good wishes for the year as my poor flowers have left unexpressed. Think anything but that I have forgotten—the memory of those last hours spent with you has hardly been absent from my thoughts. That I have not dared to tell you so, that I am goaded by the inevitable as man never was before, makes this letter the most difficult one to frame that I have ever attempted. A dozen times I have written and destroyed it, and after all I can only write the bitter word farewell."

"What is it? I cannot understand;" then brightly, "ah, how he loves me!" cried unsuspecting Berthe. "I can bear not seeing him to-day, to be made to feel this so. He will come back, and then—and then—

who would have believed that I could give Belmont such pain?"

All else forgetting, she sat and pondered over the embers of the fire until the chill of waning night sent her into the refuge of her bed. Then, remembering that she had failed to carry her vases of violets and jasmine into the antechamber for the night, she went out again into the little salon, to be met by a gush of fragrance that might have been blown on a wind from Les Amandiers.

"Belmont must have sent them," was her last waking thought; "he only could have known what would make me so exquisitely glad."

January set in bitter cold, and from all parts of the Continent came reports of impeded industry, blocked travel, starved game driven from the woods to die upon the doorstones of villages, flocks of birds dropping frozen by the wayside; of a cattle train snow-bound in the Forest of Ardennes attacked by gaunt wolves, kept at bay all night by the engineer and his assistants, intrenched in the fourgon; heroes who doubtless felt little inclined to cry out, with the duke,

> Here feel we not the penalty of Adam,
> The season's difference.

There were fierce storms, and the coasts of France and England were strewn with wrecks. But inside of indomitably gay Paris people laughed defiance at the weather. The chilled alleys of the Bois de Boulogne were filled daily with promenading crowds. Babies, strapped upon lace-trimmed pillows, were dandled by white-capped nursemaids who sat upon iron benches. Punch and Judy pursued their eternal drama with the hangman and the crocodile, before audiences eternally entertained. On every lake skaters swarmed.

Berthe, bringing back winter roses upon her pale cheeks, walked daily in the Bois, attended by her mother's maid. She missed sorely the congenial companionship of Mme. Letellier, still a prisoner at the bedside of her child. Mme. de Tersac, wrapped to the nose in furs, ventured but rarely to Villa Bois Dormant; and the young girl was obliged to decline overtures and invitations from the rest of their friends to vary her solitary life. At home, when not engaged in reading aloud to her mother from the dreary lives of saints, which formed the intellectual aliment of Mme. de Lagastine, Berthe's resource was to mount up to Mme. Letellier's deserted haunt and, kindling a few sticks with a *boule de résine* in the little stove, to read or recite the dramatic passages acquired under the tuition of her dear old friend.

Twelve days after Christmas occurs the fête cherished by Parisian *bourgeoisie*, "the

Feast of Kings." To prepare for it, Villa Bois Dormant put forth its best endeavor. Floors were rewaxed, furniture polished, lamps and candlesticks borrowed from the boarders, the salon and dining room decked with garlands of evergreen and paper flowers, card tables were set, a mysterious punch, pink and sickly, was mixed, many little cakes were ordered in from the confectioner, forests of curl papers appeared nodding over the breakfast table. Home for the holiday arrived Thérésine, the youthful granddaughter of Mme. la Propriétaire, whose advent was hailed by the old people much as that of a monkey loosed to work his will. Thérésine, aged six, had a beautiful rosy little face framed in a close-bordered cap, a voice like the enchanted flute, and the temper of an imp. Before she had been an hour under the grandmaternal roof Bois Dormant was broad awake and on its guard. Lumbering after her like an elephant, Mme. Thonet was always appearing in breathless apology for havoc wrought by Thérésine. At breakfast, Berthe's skirt, violently tugged, revealed Thérésine emerging from beneath the cloth and holding up a rosebud mouth for kisses.

"I have been pinching their legs, *ces autres*," she frankly avowed. "I love you, Mlle. Berthe, and you shall give me a spoonful of your comfitures. *Dame !* you are as pretty as the ladies in the ballet who twirl like this—so—do you see? I shall be one some day. As for those others, I will not make them my compliments, as *bonne maman* desires—they are all *vielles diablesses, va !* "

In the general excitement below stairs, Berthe escaped to her garret refuge to read a sad little note just received from Mme. Letellier.

"If I have not sought to press my lips again upon your pure brow, beloved child,

it is because between you and me is a great
gulf fixed.   I dare not speak to you of what
fills my days and nights.   If she lives, the
task to which the remainder of my life is to
be set—the work of rehabilitation—must be
worked out in silence, in the twilight of some
forgotten corner of the world; not in the
sunshine in which your steps should walk."

Berthe, feeling the truth of this to be a
pang, looked sadly about the pretty, cheerful room, kept in spotless order by rough-
handed but soft-hearted Henriette.   In a
stream of winter sunshine she sat down
with her book to study a certain *pièce*
from "Athalie," recommended by madame
for practice during the interruption to their
lessons.   With a little blue shawl huddled
around her shoulders, madame's artificial
begonias spreading their broad leaves above
her head, she knit her brows and conned
the words; then, springing to her feet,
essayed to render them with the old zeal of

the days of Les Amandiers. Back came the fire of enthusiasm which, during madame's measured teachings according to the strict canons of French art, had seemed to despairing Berthe to have forever fled. Thrilling and flushing, she declaimed the clear-cut verses to the end.

Then from behind the chintz screen at the door stepped a stranger, hat in hand. He was a rusty little man, wrapped in a paletot lined with sable fur, with a head too big for his slender body, a pair of glittering black eyes and a wide, distorted mouth.

Berthe's face burned with blushes as she made him a little courtesy, holding out her hand.

"I know you," she said. "Madame has been always hoping you would come. You are M. Bertin."

"Everybody knows the little Polichinelle," he said, with a short, harsh laugh.

6

"Everyone who honors your art recognizes the master."

Her directness pleased him. A born bully of women, the teacher of actors most in demand in Paris, Bertin liked to be faced by fearless eyes. But he did not dispense with his usual preliminary bluster.

"I suppose, then, as a seeress, you know that I came here, coaxed by a note from my old friend, Julie Letellier, to hear you try your pipe. And I've heard you. Humph!"

"Oh, monsieur!" said Berthe, a faint sickness creeping over her at thought of her display.

"I have had enough, look you," said Bertin, sitting down and taking out his snuffbox, "of deluding young women with false hopes because their eyes are bright and their tongues are supple."

"Mme. Letellier calls you a clairvoyant," said she, mustering fresh courage. "She says if there is hope you will fan it into a flame."

"Did she tell you that I refuse to accept any pupil who fails in that intuitive perception of my art without which my calling would be carthorse drudgery? *Bon!* Then what do you think of your chances at my hands?"

"What could I put into words, monsieur?" said trembling Berthe, half encouraged by something like a soft beam in his eye, "that would not seem to you bold and audacious? All my life long — nearly eighteen years—since I could speak, I have escaped into the world of your 'art,' like the girl in the story who, when cast into a pit, stretched out her hand, touched a spring, and opened a door into fairyland."

"*Tiens.* It is as Julie said. She is not *jeune fille* like most of them," murmured Bertin.

"When I go to the play I am like a foolish creature. I sit spellbound, and laugh and cry. To me it is more than music or painting to be able to interpret the burning words of a great poet or playwright and make them real."

"Oh, *la belle jeunesse!*" said Bertin, grown indulgent. "Now sit here, my child, and let me tell you that Julie Letellier has strongly enlisted my interest in you. For her, to whom in the past I am bound by many ties of friendship, I will do what I would refuse to a princess of blood royal or of finance. I will let you come to me now and again to report progress under Julie's teaching. If, as I believe, the true spark is there, we shall find it, never fear. But——"

"But?" repeated Berthe, foreseeing difficulty.

"There is one point on which I am inflexible. I no longer live to encourage the *banalité* of drawing-room recitations. If you work under me it must be for the stage."

Berthe's head swam, and her heart beat violently. Bertin smiled. The old fox knew his power.

"That is Mme. Letellier's day-dream," she stammered; "I have never dared—there are circumstances, M. Bertin."

"Exactly," said Bertin, rising and looking at his watch. "And now, as I have an appointment, I must be off. When you are ready for me, come. *Au plaisir*, mademoiselle."

The little man vanished as he had appeared—noiselessly. Longing, yet not presuming to call him back, Berthe asked herself if her interview with the celebrated artist had not been a delusion born of the most secret longing of her heart.

Caps! above all, caps! To outdo her neighbor in the matter of festal headgear was the ambition of every old lady who sat down that evening to the annual "Diner des Rois." Some of them wore helmets, others towers, some windmills, others, again, great butterflies of gauze and flowers and ribbons. The widow of the Spanish general alone came as usual in her calash of drawn black silk, in the depths of which her face looked like a little withered apple. She carried on her arm a cheap straw basket, passed around the table to receive from the plates of guests scraps and bones intended for her cat and dog at home. Madame Blanchet, ex-actress of the Gaieté, who was rolled across the courtyard in a fine chair with a hood and lamps, and was attended at table by her servants, wore a gown of stiff brocade, and her withered hand sparkled with fine rings. She, who had once held audiences entranced by her matchless skill, who had had lovers by the score, was now a mumbling old wreck, pushed and patted into shape in her chair by her page and a scowling maid. But her eyes gleamed, and she exchanged *calembours* with M. Jérome, the gallant of Bois Dormant, who wore a yellow skull cap and blew kisses to the ladies as they took their places. Mme. Thonet, her mustaches bristling with excitement under a frontispiece of lilies of the valley set in tulle, patrolled the room until fifty souls were seated around the T-shaped table. For to-night she had thrown aside domestic cares and held herself like a duchess. She was gracious to the most implacable of her daily foes, who in turn met her upon a common ground, ignoring gravies and discussing questions of the *beau monde* of *bourgeoisie.* So, too, M. Auguste, the carver, who, in evening dress with a flower in his buttonhole and with a military air, circled among the guests. No snappish rejoinders to everyday complaints about *rosbif saignant* or fowls unjustly distributed. To-morrow, in his alpaca jacket, he will go around collecting the five francs *per capita* meant to cover the extra expenses of the banquet. To-night his wit, his compliments, put everyone in spirit. Decidedly, averred the old ladies, M. Auguste was a man *très comme il faut !*

Jean, the head waiter, laden with plates from armpits to finger tips, flew like a meteor around the board. His jokes, of a personal character, were distributed impartially. The overworked maids, who were his subordinates, also forgot their aching bones, bridled, smiled, and were everywhere at once. When the feast had progressed to the stage of the dessert an awestruck hush ensued. Jean, the observed of every eye, appeared from the pantry carrying the *galette.* This, a huge cake, decorated with sugar ornaments, was cut by Mme. Thonet and handed among the guests.

Berthe's dread, that she might acquire

the queen's half of the magic bean hid in
the cake, was of brief duration. To the lot
of little Thérésine fell the great prize of the
year, and to that of old M. Jérome its companion, announcing him the king. Arm-
and-arm (or hand in hand, rather), amid a
tumult of acclamation, their majesties made
the circuit of the board, clinking glasses
with each subject and bestowing on each
a double-barreled kiss.

Thérésine, for a wonder, behaved de-
murely. Stopping by Berthe, she threw
both arms around her neck.

"Oh, how you smell sweet!" cried the
little outlaw. "But that *bonne maman* says
they will give me money and sweets, I
would not kiss one of those old and ugly!
I should rather kill them all!"

Next, seated side by side, amid a cackling
as of peacocks and macaws, their majesties
were toasted. The king having ordered,
as entailed by custom upon the sovereign,

fresh wine for all, whenever either he or
Queen Thérésine lifted glass to lips, the
company cried out, "The king drinks!"
"The queen drinks!" "Bravo! Brava!"

After a brief adjournment to the salon
for cards and coffee, the tables were dis-
mantled and pushed back; a big red-
bearded German, an agent for the sale of
Prussian beer, sat down to the piano and
dashed off a spirited galop. The irrepressi-
ble old people took the floor!

Berthe, who had left her mother for
awhile to view the merry scene, stood in a
doorway, resisting invitations to join the
dance, when Jean spoke to her from behind.

"A monsieur for ces dames, mademoiselle.
He is here waiting, as I feared to disturb
madame."

Berthe turned quickly, an ecstasy of hope
lighting up her face. It was Ludlow who
stood in the entry near the front door.

"I will not detain you," he said, noting

her change of expression. "I have just come from Mme. de Tersac, who asks if your mother will spare you to her for the 'Fête des Patineurs' next Tuesday night. I have tickets, and Comte de Barrot will go, too. I fancied the thing might amuse you to look on."

"You are very kind," said Berthe, pleased in spite of herself. "I should like it very much indeed."

But she could not do away with the first effect of her disappointment manifested in meeting him. He stopped for a few minutes to watch the old folk "foot it featly," and then abruptly took his leave.

"I suppose it is a judgment on me for fraternizing with an enemy of my country," Berthe said to herself; "but I am always uncomfortable when he is near."

By Tuesday, however, she was quite prepared to again invoke the wrath of Fate.

When she found herself with Ludlow on the edge of the illuminated pond, their chaperon having elected to remain under shelter on the bank, Berthe's vivacity got the better of her patriotism. She even forgot the gnawing anxiety at her heart to see or hear something of the still absent Belmont. With the glee of a child she threw herself into the spirit of the dazzling scene. Ludlow, in turn, charmed out of his own reserve, showed her a side he had not before displayed. She began to feel that it was time to give up the futile task of adjusting political prejudice to individual instance.

In the brilliant figures flashing upon their rounds Berthe recognized many of the personages seen at the ball of the Tuileries; last, but not least, to her girl's delight, came the Empress, more beautiful than ever in her clinging costume of sapphire blue velvet edged with plumage of the *grèbe*, skating slowly, and holding a pole supported at either end by gentlemen of the court.

Now the crowd on the pond increased to a kaleidoscope of color. Two American girls with their escorts, pausing close to Berthe, chattered incessantly about the actors in the scene.

"Carrington is the handsomest man here; I don't care if he was a rebel," said one of these young women, in answer to a remark unheard by Berthe. "He goes, of course, chiefly with that New Orleans set married into the old French families. I think Mrs. Forsyth may well congratulate herself on such a prize."

"Everybody knew she 'went' for him last season, but everybody was surprised at the announcement in *Galignani* yesterday that the wedding is set for April," said the other girl.

"Who is Mrs. Forsyth, anyhow?" asked a young man newly arrived.

"Not know Mrs. Forsyth? Why, she is the enormously rich widow of one of the partners of the banking firm Mr. Carrington is employed by—quite a romance, isn't it? Came from Mobile originally, or some one of those Southern towns—five years older than he, if she's a day. Pretty? yes, or chic rather, and such taste in dress. There they come now. Carrington returned from England Saturday, and the affair was announced at once."

Berthe, to whose consciousness these facts were conveyed with fatal accuracy, had no need to question the truth of them. Directly thereafter the couple under discussion stopped skating close to her, and Berthe recognized at once the companion of Belmont's talk in the balcony on New Year's day. A blinding light broke upon her. When Belmont, stooping to adjust Mrs. Forsyth's skate, rose again with his charming smile, to meet Berthe's eyes opened wide to his, he read, even then, something of the unalterableness of her estimate of him.

By the time they joined Mme. de Tersac that lady, who had met friends, was full of the gossip of the new engagement. Berthe's yearning hope, that no one might peep behind the curtain drawn over her slain love, was gratified by Colonel Ludlow's request that the ladies would excuse his attendance on their drive to Bois Dormant.

It was well into March, and the frowns of departing winter had been succeeded by spring warmth that brought into quick bloom the pansies and wall flowers around the court, when Mme. Letellier, released from her sad service, came back to take up her old routine at Bois Dormant. With the soldier's honors of her son and the shame and sorrow of her daughter lying alike beneath the sod, the one in far Mexico, the other in Père la Chaise, there was little left in her but a mere spark of life. But her quick perceptions took note at once

of the brave fight Berthe was making to
live down some dominating passion that
had shaken her young being as the wind
shakes a reed. With tender solicitude the
old woman gave herself to the task of awak-
ening anew Berthe's interest in her interrupted studies, and hardly a day passed that
they did not walk together in the Bois, and
return for an hour of hard work in the
chamber beneath the roof. Bertin's visit
and the girl's account of it awoke for the
first time a smile on madame's face.

"He was in earnest, my good Bertin,"
she said. "I wonder if you realized how
much that offer meant."

" I could not trust myself to think much
about it then," Berthe answered with a
sigh. "Now, again and again, it returns to
me. But oh! madame, help me to put it
from my mind. My poor mother would not
dream of consenting. I should not venture
to propose it."

Mme. de Lagastine, who, in her impassive way, had grown fond of Belmont
Carrington, lamented daily that he had quite
given them up. She consulted Mme. de
Tersac, who told her that Mr. Carrington
was now always on duty with his affianced
bride, and was little seen by any of his old
friends. The marriage, which was to take
place in April, was thought by everyone to
be a most appropriate alliance, and had
been settled between their nearest friends
long before the couple had come into
agreement on their own account. Mrs.
Forsyth, a pretty enough creature—a little
spoiled and whimsical, but no harm in her—
was the uncontrolled possessor of an income
that would put the ruined young Southerner
beyond all chances of fortune for the future.
He was handsome as a picture and everybody's favorite, had made his *coup* on first
arriving in Paris, it was whispered, but had
now fairly settled down. Truly, thought Mme.

7

de Tersac, a most suitable affair. When Berthe went out of the room the little old lady took occasion to nod her head and add :

" But for the lack of dot I have no doubt he would have offered to you for Berthe. Of course, it would have been madness for those two."

"Of course," repeated Mme. de Lagastine drearily. " I appear to recall some old talk between my husband and his neighbor, Colonel Carrington, when these children were very young. But then it was all so different."

"It is most unfortunate, Berthe's lack of dot," went on Mme. de Tersac. " There is the nephew, now, of the Comte de Barrot, an amiable young man, of excellent character, the count most willing—but, what would you have ? "

" I am cold in these raw spring days," said Berthe's mother, shivering.

"Again, I had an idea that the young Union officer, introduced to us by Barrot, admired your child greatly. But there, he has gone off to Italy, and we hear no more of him."

"Berthe de Lagastine could not ally herself with a soldier of that hated service," said Mme. de Lagastine, actually letting fall her embroidery frame. And Mme. de Tersac, who had lived in Paris during the late excitement, and cherished more lukewarm views about its issue, hastened to comfort her friend by suggesting a new stitch.

Berthe did not fail to receive from Belmont a letter written the day after the skating festival. He made no attempt at self-defense, telling her that he had been, since many months before his first visit to Rue Morny, engaged to marry Mrs Forsyth. The lady's absence in England, until after Christmas, had conspired with circumstances to bring about the present deplorable result. With all the eloquence of evident deep feeling he urged upon her to receive him for a personal explanation. Destroying this communication, she had tried to put the matter from her mind, but, as the days went on with weary tread, felt the sting of the wound increase.

It was a lovely morning in " proud-pied " April; the balm of flowers and the song of birds filled the soft spring air, when Berthe, walking in the Bois with madame, saw that the old woman's eyes expressed something she wished to speak yet dared not. The girl, conscious of a new letter thrust into the folds of her gown, that tormented her with beseechings to see Belmont once again, sat down beneath an oak tree in a quiet spot, and tried to think what she should do.

" My own Berthe," began the French-woman timidly, " sympathy you have, but you need counsel. May I speak ? "

"If you only knew what a struggle is going on within me," cried the girl passionately. "I seem to have lost my sense of right or wrong. Oh, but I cannot tell you— I cannot! I should die of shame!"

The words were no sooner spoken than repented of. A dull red burned on the old woman's swarthy cheek. Her head dropped upon her chest, and her eyes brimmed with hot tears.

"That fate is not for you, my child," said madame brokenly. "No, never mind, it gives me the courage I required. Berthe, can you bear a blow? Try, then, to understand why every impulse of my nature is against your trusting him who has won your love."

Berthe started fiercely, as if a serpent had writhed across her path. She ventured an imploring glance into madame's face, and read there the blasting truth.

"Élise, too, loved him—she believed in

him ; because he forsook her she cast away the remnants of her miserable life," the mother stammered, pressing her hands together in the effort at self-repression.

Berthe did not question her. She only sat in a kind of dumb despair. Her thoughts, roving over her brief, eventful life, recalled what, long ago, her old nurse Clarisse had cried out from the anguish of a life-long grief, " Dey cawn't help deyselves, dem Carrin'tons. He's got blood in his veins dat will surely bring misery to dem dat loves him."

"Oh, Mammy Clarisse!" the girl said within herself, " I'm glad you didn't live to know I was to suffer with the rest."

She saw Belmont again, unseen by him, when with Mme. de Tersac she went to a concert given for the benefit of the exiled Poles in Paris by their aristocratic country-women of the Hôtel Lambert. In the center of the large *salle*, at Mrs. Forsyth's side, amid an animated group of the beautiful women and picturesque men whose velvet-soft dark eyes and dazzling tint of skin betokened their nationality, Belmont Carrington was sitting. He had turned away from his betrothed, and was talking with a little fair-haired prince of an ancient Polish house, whose mother, a great lady of Spain, bent graciously toward him from the other side.

During the hush attending a performance on the piano by the Princess Marcelline Czartoryska accompanied by a chosen orchestra, Mrs. Forsyth, her throat wrapped with strings of priceless pearls, her pretty head overweighted by an aigret of gems, whispered to Belmont, who gave her no answering smile. He had lapsed into reverie, evidently not of an enlivening nature, and Mrs. Forsyth, in token of her displeasure, promptly devoted herself to the man upon her right. At the first interval Carrington arose and withdrew from the hall, and from her modest corner Berthe caught one final glimpse of him standing, jaded and unsmiling still, in the doorway, behind a crowd of golden youths, idlers and butterflies, whose rank he was now to join for good. That he had changed, that he was not the happy, buoyant Belmont of a few months back, she could not doubt. In her dread of encountering his wandering eye she shrank behind Mme. de Tersac, and effaced herself with a fan, until the concert came to a close.

The experience of this evening, however poignant, was destined to be swept away by one more momentous in consequence. Reaching Villa Bois Dormant, Berthe found her mother suffering from an attack of heart trouble, of which she had had one or two premonitory hints. Two days later Mme. de Lagastine died, and Berthe, casting herself into the arms of feeble Mme. Letellier, realized that she and the great world were now looking at each other face to face. The immediate cause of Mme. de Lagastine's seizure, it was thought, was a letter from Mr. Duval, in New Orleans, informing her of the final shrinkage of the sources of her income, which would reduce the sum henceforth to be counted on to a pittance insufficient for their support.

At the first news of Berthe's loss came kind Mme. de Tersac, proffering to the girl a home until her affairs could be put into shape. Other friends called, and the Southern colony bestirred itself with cordial tokens of regard. Laid in her coffin, poor Mme. de Lagastine looked almost as in life; but when the still form was shut finally from human sight, Berthe's lonely heart ached to bring back her solitary prop.

Driving to Mme. de Tersac's apartment from the funeral, and consenting to let her friend go on alone to Bois Dormant for necessary oversight of what was left there, Berthe mounted many flights, solitary and heart-sick, to be admitted by sympathetic Marie, madame's maid.

There was tea in waiting, Marie said, but if mademoiselle would prefer a *tisane* of *eau de fleur d'oranger* to calm the nerves, Marie would mix one before she should see the gentleman. What gentleman, did mademoiselle ask? *Dame!* Marie could not say, not being in the habit of answering the bell; but a gentleman, young and handsome, who had positively declared that he must see mademoiselle, with or without madame, as soon as she returned from the last melancholy duties to *feu madame la mère de mademoiselle.*

Berthe's heart gave a great leap when she went into Mme. de Tersac's tiny sitting-room. Haggard, pallid, love pleading in his eyes, Belmont Carrington stood before her.

" I was there at the cemetery and at the church," he said in a hoarse voice. " Could you think that I would let you bear this alone? For the sake of old times, for Les Amandiers, I could not keep away."

"It has been a great shock," Berthe began mechanically, and stopped, choking. On a billow of love her heart went out to answer the look in his face. Not moving toward her, but beseeching her by gaze, he held out his arms. For a moment she stood trembling, fascinated, sorely tempted to weep away her lonely sorrows on his breast —then drew back with a shudder.

"Oh, you are cruel!" she said. "You would make me like yourself."

"Berthe, hear me," he whispered in her ear. "Anything is better than to live a lie. You and I love one another. I have done my best to be true to her; it is a miserable failure. Last week, when I sat at her side listening to music, the thought of that Christmas mass came between us and—I believe I hated her."

"Hush, hush, you pain me beyond words," she said imploringly.

"Pain you? When it is because of the vast desire I have to comfort you, to take you into my life and surround you with my love that I am driven to speak now? Come to me, Berthe. Be my wife, let the world wag as it may. What can a frail young thing do in a solitude like yours? Duval has written to me of your new embarrassments. Let me care for you, share my lot with you. Marry me to-day, to-morrow, if you will."

"But—I don't understand. You are—now—free?" she stammered.

"I admit no ties but the one that God has made between your heart and mine," he said with a clouding brow.

Berthe clasped her hands over her face and tried to think. If in the first strong temptation her sense of right had tottered, it was still firm on a foundation he could not understand. Being true to her loftier instincts, it was impossible that she should yield. But in the somber, insistent man beside her she had met with a new element in her girlish experience. It seemed to her that another creature was looking from Belmont's eyes.

"Berthe, what good can you do by condemning our two lives to misery?" he went on, dreading her silence. "If you like, I can be transferred to New Orleans, and our home shall be far from the memories of Paris. Some day, when we are rich, we shall go back to Les Amandiers. Do you remember that alley of oleanders down which I ran to save you? To walk there with your hand in mine—Berthe, you are cold—you tremble—are you faint?"

"Listen to me," she said, rising to put the width of the room between them. "I've let you speak because I am weak, maybe—too weak even to resent affront. No, don't interrupt me. I don't mean to resent it now.

I'm not going to pretend to hide what you've
made me feel. I think there can never have
been a girl who suffered more in being deceived. Whatever I suffer henceforth, it
can't be worse than that. Even if I considered you honorably free, it would not
alter the mistrust I should have of
you."

"Ah, how you can sting!" he cried.
"Who would think that a young creature
like you would be one of the judicial, unfor-
giving sort?"

"I can forgive," she went on more gently,
seeing him deeply wounded. "But long
before we met here to-day I had made up
my mind that I dared not trust."

"What are women put in the world for
but to be angels of pity and gentleness, if
they are not angels of the other sort?
Why can't you say: 'He sinned, he offended
me, he cut me in my tenderest part, but he
loves me and I love him.' Love like ours

ought to be the first law of the universe, after love for God. You stand there just like a sister who has resolved to put on the black veil. Only think what a glorious thing life is when you come out into the broad light. If you want a mission, reform me. Take my burdens with my love. For I do love you, Berthe. You have got hold of the fibers of my heart."

"No matter what came, there would always be that between us," she said resolutely. "If I live to be an old woman I could never get back just what you have taken from me. At the moment when inclined to think most kindly of you, I should find myself calling on you to give me back my lost faith, my girl's joy in loving."

"You are too young to cherish such thoughts. Come to me, and I will make your life a glory and a beauty such as you never dreamed of, Berthe."

"You have everything upon your side," she said, with a pathos that struck him with compassion. "And I, who am, as you say, a young girl with no one to counsel me, no experience of the world, only my instincts to guide me, am not good at such an argument. But, such as I am, I have lived, I have thought and weighed and measured things. It is my unhappiness, not my fault, that I do not now feel as I did five months ago."

"You are indeed a wonder," he answered, goaded by her calm.

"I am very tired," she said, dropping into a chair and throwing back the long crape veil that had fallen half across her face. This gesture reminded Carrington, with a shock, of what he had forgotten. He bowed in silence, and turned to go out of the room.

"Not in anger?" she exclaimed, with a touch of her old impulsiveness. "Won't

you take the hand of your playmate and bid
her a kind good-by?"

"Berthe, let me be something in your
life." he cried, coming back to her side im-
petuously.

"Not now," she said, very low. He took
her fingers in his warm clasp, but she did not
stir toward him. Then Belmont moved to
the door. With his hand upon the knob, he
looked back and met her gaze. Her sad
eyes, her slight figure in the mourning dress,
the proud poise of her head under its brown
coronal of hair, might haunt his memory—
but they did not suggest to him that Berthe
would change.

Some years after this episode Bertin's
pupil, Miss St. Felix, made her first courtesy
behind the footlights in New York. Her
American birth and parentage, her beauty
and talent, even the old story about her
great-grandmother, the French actress, had
8

been discussed in the newspapers for a year
before her *début* in her native land. The
disclosure of her ancestor's calling, which
afflicted no one living save Mme. de
Tersac, inclined Parisians to look favorably
upon Bertin's clever *protégée*, and her appearance in various modest rôles of the
French drama had been well received. The
old master, who watched her like a hawk,
had taken care that her dramatic ascent had
been made by safe degrees. When the dis-
turbances in France afforded her a good
opportunity to accept an engagement in
America, Bertin, with fierce begrudging, lent
her to the English-speaking stage, "as an
experiment," he said. During her novitiate
of hard work she had remained as if clois-
tered under Mme. Letellier's charge at
Bois Dormant. The ex-actress, whose
youth was renewed in her, trotted about
after Berthe and waited in the wings with
perfect satisfaction. On her first appear-

ance as an *ingénue* Berthe's private claque
had consisted of a deputation from Bois
Dormant, headed by M. Jérome with
his skullcap and snuffbox, and including
Mme. Thonet, M. Auguste, and as many
of the ancients as could sally forth to chirp
approval. The success of her efforts being
duly sanctioned by the *habitués* of a favorite
theater, Mrs. Belmont Carrington, who happened to be in the audience that night, remarked afterward to her husband—who had
happened to stay at home—that he must
really make it a point to go to see that little
Miss What's-her-name from New Orleans, as
Angèle in " Le Monde d'Aujourdhui."

Now Berthe had tried her wings in the
broad empyrean. She came back into her
little gas-lighted dressing room in the New
York theater, after the third act, stunned
by her success. While madame and the
maid hovered over her toilet for the final
scene, she appeared to be restlessly looking

for something that had not come. A box, handed in, was opened eagerly. She blushed like a schoolgirl when she drew out from a bed of violets a bunch of southern jasmine. As there was still some little time before her last entrance upon the scene, she dismissed her attendants and sat plunged in thought. When Mme. Letellier came in again she found that Berthe had fastened the jasmine on her breast, and was looking at herself in the mirror with a somewhat melancholy smile.

"But you, who never wear flowers upon the scene, my Berthe!" exclaimed madame, noting it.

"I shall always wear this flower," Berthe answered.

When, after a *finale* that left no room to doubt of the enthusiastic temper of the audience in favor of the actress, Berthe went out to get into her carriage, she found Ludlow waiting at the stage door.

"Is it true?" he said, "I can't half believe it. I feel like a beggar who has plucked a star to wear in his buttonhole."

"I have something more to give you than I had at first," she answered. "And you deserve everybody's best. The only thing I fear is that people will say I have done this to avenge history."

Happily, people say very little of any sort about Berthe in these latter days. Mme. de Tersac died rejoicing, Mme. Letellier not so assured in satisfaction at her marriage and consequently brief career upon the stage. Little Bertin was, of course, furious over it, but when he fell fighting like a Trojan in defense of Paris in 1871, the number of Berthe's lawful critics was notably reduced. Ludlow, of course, came in for the lion's share of unfavorable comment bestowed by society upon the situation, but as he was well known for cool indifference to trivial opinion, and as the couple set themselves to live their united life after their own fashion in a community where all sensations are transient, gossip soon left them for a more shining mark.

"In each of our lives the seasons are mingled as in the golden age. . . . . Fruit and blossom hang together . . . harvest and springtime are continually one." In the fullness of contentment long withheld, Berthe's glad youth came back to reward her husband.

A THORN IN HIS CUSHION.

"WELL, I've obtained the chariot for a day," Dale said, settling himself comfortably back in an easy-chair, representing the editorial throne of a certain monthly magazine—a place which it did not occur to him to think himself lacking in any requisite to fill; "the question is, Shall I be merciful and refrain from 'setting the world on fire'?"

Looking up, the young editor caught a rather severe glance from a very black-a-vised photograph of Thomas Carlyle hanging on the wall above the desk; an expression at once convicting him of untimely levity. Pulling himself together, he proceeded to the work in hand—turning over and sorting a series of MSS. left from the last labor of Hercules of his departed chief.

For, on the morning of one of those "drippy, slippy, nippy" mornings in March, of which New York alone is capable, the editor of the *Cosmos* had betaken himself, his weak lung, his wife, baby, etc., to a train in Jersey City, bound for Florida. And as luck would have it, on the same day, the second in command had succumbed to a sudden cold, threatening evils that would hold him house-bound for a week. Therefore it was that upon Mr. Henry Hillhouse Dale, junior in office as in years, fell the honors of the editorial hour. All things considered, it was a surprisingly short time since he had been called on to perform the same duties for that respected and long-lived periodical, the Yale *Lit.* Harry's mother, widow of the late Judge Dale, for

many years a most estimable citizen of the
pretty leafy town in Berkshire where she
still dwelt, thought it was only a just recog-
nition by Fate of her boy's surprising tal-
ents that had carried him so briskly along
the literary path.

However self-satisfied, Dale soon relapsed
into the inevitable paralysis of hope that
besets the reader of average MSS. One
contribution after another, from authors
convinced that their right to enlighten
society through the columns of the *Cosmos*
had been revealed to them by a handwriting
of celestial fire, was tossed aside. The usual
callers—important, insistent, pathetic, un-
sparing, or business-like—had been inter-
viewed. There was within Dale a still small
voice pleading for lunch, unanswered, and
there yet remained to him for examination
a woman's MS.

"Here goes," he said, suppressing the
anticipatory groan : "I begin to understand

the resignation that routine work must have inspired in those headsmen in the Reign of Terror.   A story!   Yes, of course, and twice too long, to begin with.   Luckily her ink is black and her manuscript doesn't roll.   How well she dots her i's.   Ha! that's not bad. The description's too diffuse; but she's got a grip on her idea.   Let me see, who *is* the contributor in the case?"

He turned back to the note accompanying the parcel, running his eye lazily over its pages—a true girl's letter, couched between coaxing and command.   This was her first contribution to any magazine.   In notifying her of his acceptance, the editor might address "Miss E. T., care of Mme. Leblanc, No. 3001 West Thirty-sixth Street."

"Fresh as Bermuda cucumbers!" Dale said, smiling.   But he did not put aside the manuscript.   Like the good and conscientious editor he was, the young man picked it up again.   Whatever might have been the

faults of E. T.'s style, and they were plenti-
ful, there was a true ring in her sentiment, a
sparkle in her unjaded humor, that gushed
like a spring under the palms of the editorial
oasis. It smoothed Dale's wrinkled front,
and left him in as good a humor as can be
expected of an empty man, who has gone
luncheonless till 3 P.M. One thing Dale did
not do. He did not bow-string Miss E. T.
upon the spot. He merely pigeon-holed
her, intending to write her a personal note
upon the morrow.

Next day, when Dale's thoughts were a
thousand miles away from Miss E. T., she
called. The young man from the outermost
circle of office guardians, who announced
the visitors, merely, however, presented
to Dale a card announcing that Mme.
Leblanc, approved by the Society of Deco-
rative Art, gave lessons in china painting,
tapestry painting, macramé lace, and ar-
rasene embroidery, either at the residence

of pupils or at her own house, No. 3001 West Thirty-sixth Street.

"That's the *old* lady, a French one, sir," said Wilson, faintly grinning. "There's another one, sir, and they say they will keep the editor only one moment."

"Show them in, then ; and mind, call me in ten minutes, Wilson."

A moment later the portal of multicolored glass slid noiselessly upon its groove to admit the callers. First, Mme. Leblanc, habited like an empress of the lyric stage, her vast person gleaming with jet, her bonnet beplumed after a fashion recently introduced under the style of "Enterrement de la première classe."

Behind her, a slight young thing in a close-fitting brown frock, with a veil of brown tissue half drawn across a peach-tinted face, a mouth made for laughter and for kissing, just now rather woe-struck and drooping at the corners. Dale's eye took all this in while addressing itself politely to the exhortation of Mme. Leblanc, who had come, she informed him, to inquire about a story sent by her young friend, Miss E. T., now some weeks since.

"Your young friend is probably little accustomed to the slow grinding of editorial mills," answered Dale, attempting to assume an air at once impersonal and fatherly; and hurrying on he tried to pave the way toward extracting the MS. from its pigeon-hole, and conveying it back to Miss E. T. with all the grace and ease of which he felt himself to be master.

"But are you sure the editor has seen it?" here interposed the girl, with a bridling of her small head that seemed not to accord with the shabby gentility of her protector.

"I am the editor," Dale answered, somewhat nettled; "by to-morrow this story would have been in your hands again, had you not honored me to-day.   To read it has given me pleasure, and I sincerely wish it might do so to the many readers of our magazine—but——"

"There is no hope for me?" she cried, with the upbraiding of a child in her soft voice, and to Dale's dismay two bright tears rolled down from under the brown-tissue veil upon the flushing cheeks.

Wilson's arrival at that crisis was a boon for which Dale afterward rewarded the young man by the unexplained present of a couple of theater tickets.

"Talk about thorns in the editorial cushion," Dale remarked, when on a visit that evening to his convalescent superior. "Dear old Thackeray knew what he was about when he wrote that essay. To have a pretty girl, who, no doubt, expected to feed several widowed mothers from the proceeds, come into your private office, and cry over her rejected manuscript — by Jove! another minute, and I should have been wiping away her poor dear little tears."

" It's high time I turned out again," remarked the other grimly, reaching over for a cigar.

Next day, what should Dale do but settle himself squarely to the task of writing " E. T." a letter, which should embody all the disinterested good advice on the art of modern composition, to supply the demand of buyers of modern magazines, his experience could suggest. It was an excellent letter— Harry felt with pride—a letter worthy to be hektographed and retained in the office for similar occasions—a letter that would be eagerly bought up by a syndicate to print as the official utterance of an expert. Might it not, therefore, serve as a peace-offering to the sorely afflicted Miss E. T., whose look, as she retired with her rejected treasure, he could not yet forget ? Poor girl ! poor girl ! No doubt—everything pointed to the conclusion—she had staked an infinity of hope upon her hapless venture, and it was curious to see how long those round, pellucid tears had held together before dissolving on the peach-bloom of her cheek. He had never seen a woman cry becomingly before. . . . . Well, of all the driveling idiots !

Finding himself *tête-à-tête* with a post-box, Dale dropped into it his letter to E. T., and dismissed—or thought he did—the subject from his mind.

A week later he had the curiosity to turn his steps across Sixth Avenue, into the midway region of one of those cross-streets that begin so well and finish so shabbily. Within the border-line of decrepit respectability, he found the house designated by the card of Mme. Leblanc. It was a recently built structure, of brick with a plaster of brown stone, and cheap colored glass bedecked the transom of the front door—a " flat " house of the most depressing pattern. In

the vestibule were rows of speaking trumpets, with the card of the owner of each
tacked above it. Mme. Leblanc lived on
the fifth floor. He looked about him hesi-
tatingly. On one side of the house was a
German grocery; on the other the entrance
to a stable. In the dirty street, dirty children were wrangling at their play beneath
the grocer's wagon. A boy, carrying a load
of kindling-wood, jostled him roughly.
Dale, who was uncertain what he came
there to do, found himself the object of
speculation from frowsy lodgers who passed
in and out. As the door opened, a gush
of onions, cooking, rushed forth upon the
breeze.

"Poor E. T.," sighed Dale, and turned
away.

During the spring following this trivial
episode, Dale's time and attention were ab-
sorbed by weightier things. " Poems, by
9

Henry Hillhouse Dale," a modest volume,
bound in olive green, with orange lettering,
had made its appearance before a moder-
ately startled world.   Among the varied
comments upon his book, Harry held sacred
a letter from his mother, that had drifted
down to him from her bowery home, as an
apple-blossom falls to earth.

"Oh! my dear, darling boy," the letter
ran, " how shall I ever tell you my feelings
when I cut the string around your precious
book?   My hand trembled so, my heart
beat, and I couldn't help looking up at
your father's picture for sympathy.   In my
delight over its present beautiful appearance, I will confess to you that the galley
slips you first sent gave me many pangs.
I couldn't imagine how the gold-winged
butterfly of my ambition was to emerge
from that dingy chrysalis.   O, Harry, the
poems are lovelier than ever!   Everybody
must think so.   You will be famous, and I

shall be so proud—prouder than before, if such a thing can be—of my own, clever, handsome, loving son."

Dale began by smiling broadly, and ended by wiping his eyes. He read the letter while waiting for his dinner in an Italian restaurant, and his sentiment was cut short by a dish of *macaroni au gratin*, briskly deposited before him. By and by he took up the sheet again.

" It is so beautiful in Hillsboro, now ; you can't imagine a more lovely June. The old syringa bushes over the front gate look as if a snow-drift were upon them ; the meadow is full of big daisies and buttercups ; the robins sing from morning until night. Do get off for a Sunday, soon, and run up to me, my lad. . . . .

" And now for our village gossip. It is quite true the old Gardiner homestead has been sold to one of your New York capital-ists, a Mr. Jeremiah Thorne."

" Thorne, Baker & Evans, the sugar people," ejaculated Dale. " Alas! for poor old
Hillsboro! the Egyptians will despoil her."

" Although workmen have been occupied
in overhauling the house for some months
past, the name of the buyer has never come
out till this week. You remember my telling you of the young people of the Thorne
family last year. They had rooms at the
hotel, with their governess and maids, while
the father and mother, and oldest sister, were
in Europe. This summer they have come
again, the mamma with them, a faded, over-
dressed little person, who drives about the
village streets in a victoria with showy horses
and clanking chains. They are to move
into the old house when the furniture is in
order. The father, who comes up on Saturday evening by the late train, and goes back
on Monday morning, looks as if he were on
springs, so nervous and restless he is. It is
hard to believe that pair the parents of the

charming children with whom I have already made acquaintance—shall I tell you how?

"Last summer, one of the little lads came up the garden path, as bold as Julius Cæsar, to tell me he had thrown his ball across my palings, and broken one of my tall, white lilies from the stalk, and that he wished to beg my pardon.

"'As for the lilies, there are plenty of them,' I said, smiling; 'but there are not many little boys who think of an old woman's feelings for her flowers.'

"'Oh! but I didn't,' he cried out. 'It was my sister Nora, who told me I *must* come, and Nora's such a jolly girl, you know. She's out there walking along, waiting for me, and I must go.'

"'Take Nora this lily and another, won't you?' I said, putting the flowers in a rather grimy little paw. He ran off with a merry 'Thank you,' and I saw him join a girl, who bent down and kissed him as he handed

her the lilies. A Sunday or two later I
met Master Tom Thorne with his sister
coming out of church, and we struck up
a conversation based upon the lilies,
Until the other day I saw no more of
them. Last week Tom and Nora, accompanied by a splendid collie dog, passed by
our house, and the dog, dashing in, threat-
ened to devastate my poppy bed. To call him
away brought the two young people to our
gate, and as I was working among my flowers,
they stopped awhile to aid me, Tom with
more zeal than discretion, I'm afraid. All
this time I haven't told you that Nora is
a darling; sweet, unspoiled, impulsive, just
what I should have wished your poor sister
to have grown up had she lived. It is incredible that she should belong to those
Thornes, who are essentially commonplace
and self-important people. This girl lives
her own life apart from theirs, it's plain.
She is fond of nature, out-door sports, of

dogs, of the company of her brother Tom.
She is well poised, mentally, and 'hath a
pretty wit.' Altogether, her society is
agreeable to me, and, if this is not an old
woman's vanity, I fancy mine is to her.
She caught sight of the shelves full of by-
gone books in our sitting-room, and begged
my leave to look at them. Since then
hardly a day has passed that I have not
had her at the house. What *will* you say
now to the old lady's romantic attachment?"

Next week Harry's letter from Hillsboro
contained more details of his mother's new-
found friendship :

"What more natural than that our conversation should frequently turn upon *you?*
Nora looked at your old college photograph,
but said little in comment. Of course, that
was because it never did you justice, dear.
With your present beard and mustache,
too, it can hardly be said to resemble you.
When, however, she came to take up my

copy of your poems, and saw what you had
written on the fly leaf—that dear inscription
offering your first fruits of poetry to *me*—
her face brightened.   Was it possible that I
was the mother of—this 'Henry Hillhouse
Dale' was the 'Harry' who—why, for a
year past she had been cutting everything
signed by that name out of the newspapers
and pasting it in her scrap-book!   When
your poems were announced, she had sent
an immediate order to her bookseller to forward to her a copy of the book as soon as it
was published."

"That's tangible!" said Dale.   "I like
that kind of an admirer.   Unfortunately,
the crop is limited.   I like her scrap-book,
too."

"She is immensely interested in the *Cosmos* magazine; says her father has taken it
for years, and approves of it as a distinct
business success of a pure American type,
although she has never seen him do much

more than glance over the pictures. She asked me all sorts of questions about your staff—the editor-in-chief, particularly. I said I had never met him, but believed him to be a most worthy gentleman. Next, she wanted to know if he is married, and I told her yes, to such a pretty wife, and that their twins are, to judge from what you said, a most wonderful pair of children."

Dale's mid-summer holiday with his mother was spent at a seashore resort upon the Jersey coast, instead of, as usual, at Hillsboro, and it was not until late in September that he again visited his home. The autumn fires had begun to kindle in swamp and forest, and all nature was in readiness to celebrate that season which makes of Berkshire one of earth's rarest garden spots. Harry knew every station on the dusty, dislocating Housatonic Railway—every shoulder

of the hills, every brawling torrent, every
manufactory and wayside village was dear
to him.   When he reached home, it was
with a school-boy's fervor that he threw his
arms around his mother's neck and kissed
her.   He had walked ahead of the lumbering
stage, had burst in, unannounced, and, in
his glee, did not perceive the presence
of a young woman, who had quietly with-
drawn as he entered his mother's sitting
room.

"Harry! why, Harry!" cried breathless
Mrs. Dale. Then looking around, she
added: "How nice that you should meet
Nora in this informal way.   Well, she's gone
by the side porch, after all the trouble she's
taken to arrange the flowers.   It's really too
bad."

Harry, politely sympathetic, did not feel
particularly sorry to miss the encounter.
He looked around him full of satisfaction in
the old room, so fresh and smart with new

chintzes, and with late roses in every vase and corner.

" It never looked so nice," he said, complacently.

"Yes, we've worked hard," Mrs. Dale answered, with a sagacious nod. "Nora put all sorts of ideas into my head about turning and twisting furniture, and scattering odds and ends around the tables. Girls are all that way, nowadays, it seems. O Harry! you must like Nora, if it's only for the sake of the poor sister you lost."

A method of reasoning not very clear to Dale, but he acquiesced, lazily, and before the day was out, found himself even wondering when the much-bepraised Miss Nora would show up. To Mrs. Dale's regret, the young lady was out on horseback when the widow called next morning, in due form, with her son. The same ill luck attended several attempted meetings until, out of patience, Mrs. Dale sent a note containing an invitation to tea, so couched that Miss Thorne could not, in courtesy, decline it.

At the appointed hour, therefore, enter Miss Nora Thorne, her head well up, a flush upon her cheeks, her erect, young figure attired with what seemed to her entertainers rather unusual splendor for a cottage banquet. As Dale took the cold hand she held out to him, he became conscious of a familiar line of lips and chin, of a pearly texture of the skin around them, of a certain dimple lying in wait for an opportunity to appear near the left-hand corner of the mouth.

"You — *you* are not E. T.?" he stammered, with all a man's bluntness.

"I am Eleanora Thorne," the girl said with dignity.

"What *do* you mean, Harry?" asked the puzzled widow.

"A stupid mistake of mine, that's all,"

Dale said, smothering a strong desire to laugh. To Nora it was evidently not a joke.

A week of ambient atmosphere, of un-premeditated meetings, of rambles in the rainbow woods, of talks beside the dropping embers in the widow's sitting room, broke down the barrier, as not a year's acquaintance in city limits could have done.

"Chiefly because you have never asked me," said Nora to Dale one evening at the hour of blind man's holiday, when his mother had left the two young people to-gether for a space, "I will tell you about that adventure of mine. First of all, I honestly believed my story was a good one."

"So say we all of us," answered Dale, but not with malice.

"Then, my father, who was rather proud of my taking so many first-composition prizes at school, told me he would give me $500 for our 'Baby Shelter' in New York (I'm the secretary, you know, and a lot of us girls work hard for it) if I could succeed in getting an article accepted by a first-class magazine. Naturally, I thought of the *Cosmos*."

"Thanks. So many writers do," murmured Dale.

"Oh! You needn't be sarcastic. I don't mind you, now. It was only when I thought you were *the* editor. The real thing, you know. Well, I wrote that story, and polished it and copied it and sent it, and then, while I was waiting to hear about it, I thought I should *die*. I did not dare take anyone at home into my confidence, and so I sent for old Leblanc, the teacher of our china-painting class at school, the best old soul. They say she supports an ancient father (exactly like old Time, with a velvet cap on) in her rooms, somewhere on the

West Side, and that she has to feed and dress him like a child."

" And I, who believed you to be a scion of the house Leblanc! Why, the sentiment I wasted in that vestibule!"

"What are you talking about? Oh! Yes, I remember your letter; *that* letter came through madame to me."

"Why do you say '*that* letter' with such a sniff of contempt? It appears to me, as I remember it, that letter was a model."

" Of conceit and condescension, certainly," said Miss Thorne, with much amusement. " I don't believe patronage could farther go. One might have supposed you to be as old as old Monsieur Leblanc. But then, luckily, I had seen you."

" The recollection seems to have afforded you solace in your trial," said Harry, piqued.

" I don't deny what you said was clever. Perhaps it was just, although it did seem to

me rather ridiculous that the only part you
singled out for praise was the passage-at-
arms between Agnes and her great-aunt
about the Sunday bonnet."

"Yes, the Sunday bonnet," repeated
Dale, who was just then wandering a little
in admiration of the way Nora's loose hair
curled in fluffy rings upon the back of her
neck. "Oh—yes; as I said, the Sunday
bonnet. That was natural, sprightly, a bit
of everyday life photographically repro-
duced. What I told you then, I mean.
You have undoubted power of expression.
With years of practice, you might in time
come to write acceptable stories for our
magazines. But, oh! there are so many
people who write acceptable stories, and so
few like you, who——"

"Mr. Dale!" said Nora, interrupting him,
"I can't think what is the matter with you.
You are not a bit like yourself, generally.
Your mind is not in the least fixed on the

subject of our talk. Now, please brace up
and pay me some attention."

" Good gracious ! " said Harry helplessly.
" That's exactly what I'm doing. Too much
for my own good."

"I want to start fresh with you, and ask
you to be my friend and helper. I believe
your letter, hateful as it was to take—like a
particularly big pill—did me good. I don't
agree to give up scribbling. Perhaps I may
write one good, short story, publish it in the
Cosmos, and then expire of pride. But I
don't even promise that——"

" Promise only to enchant me as you do
now, forever," said the irrelevant young
man, with deplorable impetuosity. Nora's
heart gave a great rejoicing bound. She did
not believe her ears. He was outrageous,
deserving of instant punishment. Her over-
powering desire was to jump up and run out
of the room. But she did nothing of the
kind.

10

Dale went back to town glorified. The "thorn in his cushion" had been made to blossom like a rose.

As far as heard from, Nora has never become a contributor to the *Cosmos* magazine, unless, perhaps, indirectly—a state of things seeming to give equal satisfaction to all concerned.

MR. CLENDENNING
PIPER.

MR. CLENDENNING PIPER will be remembered as the aspirant to fashion who, appearing at one or two places of summer resort a few years since, the proprietor of a well-set-up four-in-hand, spilt various confiding parties of guests, sprained the ankles of at least three women, and reduced several promising young dudes to the condition of football champions after a college game, before public opinion prevailed on him to lay the ribbons down and part with his outfit at such price as it would fetch. Mr. Piper, while he is written down a resident and

voter of New York, has been little seen
there during the season when the society
of which he desires to form a part is engaged in its dizzy round of diurnal pleasures. Although no one, to gaze upon his
cherubic proportions and cheeks perma-
nently blushing like lady apples, would give
him credit for weakness of the lungs, he
has thrown out a hint to the effect that his
physicians insist upon his wintering in
Florida; and to the Oriental splendors of
the Ponce de Leon he has accordingly
allied himself not infrequently. Ill-natured
people say that he avoids New York because he has failed to get into certain
clubs for which his small soul yearns; but
then people are so ill-natured! Those who
have whispered these legends oftenest, it
must be observed, have eaten Mr. Piper's
dinners, drunk his wines, and used his
horses whenever bidden to do so *outside* of
the metropolis.

Reputed to be the heir of ancestral mil-
lions, Mr. Piper might have been, nay is, a
planet of the first importance on the hori-
zons below the empyrean where he aspires
to rule. " What ! You don't know Mr.
Clendenning Piper?" inquire in astonishment the denizens of cities where the little
man has managed to get a foothold in society, of their friends within the penetralia
of New York. " Why, down here he is no
end of a swell. Mrs. Druid Park, under
the impression that he belonged to your
smart set, you know, had him at her
autumn house party. And the Schuylkills
took him on their yacht, and the F. F.
Richmonds got him to lead their cotillon
when they brought out their oldest girl,"
etc., etc., etc. And still the portals Mr.
Piper longs to enter in New York open not !

The little episode of his checkered career
which I am about to divulge had its origin
in an expedition at Bar Harbor, arranged

by him in honor of a certain Mrs. Penfold,
greatly in vogue that season upon the
plank-walk, in hotel verandas, and on the
rattling parties by buckboard to sup at
Somesville, across the island, and drive home
by light of the moon. Mrs. Penfold, like
Mr. Piper, was a newcomer of antecedents
vague—a widow of several years' standing,
not particularly young, or pretty, or rich,
and not accomplished, save in the one exquisite art of making herself agreeable to the
person with whom it was her lot to be temporarily thrown.   Added to this she had large,
dark eyes, a knack of telling fortunes of the
most flattering elasticity of bounds, and
waltzed so well as to accentuate her com-
plaisance in allowing Mr. Piper, who spins
like a teetotum, to take her out for many a
turn at the Kebo Valley dances.   Like Mr.
Piper, Mrs. Penfold knew herself to be as yet
a burr on the outer skirts of society.   The
tabbies of the hotel said many unkind things

of her flirtations, and she was as yet unrecognized by the social autocrats who make or mar. Like him, too, she had industry, persistence in shedding snubs, good temper, and a secret determination to get on. Recognizing fellowship, Mr. Piper felt at first inclined to avoid rather than to fraternize with this doubtful little person; but finding himself seated at her table at the Merry-Go-Round Hotel, and exposed daily to the appeal of her pathetic eyes and ways, his reserve melted. When his new naphtha launch came around from Boston, he went so far as to ask Mrs. Penfold to preside over his initial party for a run about Frenchman's Bay.

Passing over the details of this entertainment, when Mr. Piper, like a grand pasha, surrounded himself chiefly with fair females, and a couple of men so insignificant that rivalry was not to be feared; when, clad in all the latest coquetries of male nautical attire, he stood like Pleasure at the Prow; when, after the champagne and sandwiches and marsh mallows had been exhausted, it was discovered that the naphtha had followed suit, and that it was necessary, then several miles beyond Bald Rock, to row the launch to shore—it will suffice to say that Mrs. Penfold's amiability, her two Spanish songs, her conundrums and her fortune-telling carried the day, and Mr. Piper fell in love.

Everybody predicted that the wise little widow would, before Christmas, have the lawful spending of Mr. Piper's shekels; but no engagement was announced. For reasons best known to herself she kept his proposal at arm's length. He and she, and the gay revelers of a season, drifted away from Bar Harbor long before the first leaves had left the trees, and nobody knew that Mrs. Penfold had given her Piper leave to speak definitely, with the hope of a not unfavorable reply, during the first week of

December, at her apartments in New York.
Mr. Piper sighed at his probation, but acquiesced. He was, by that time, bowled by
the tender passion completely off his feet.
What to do with the intervening months,
for she had exacted that he was to keep his
distance from New York, he could not tell.
So he got aboard a steamer, turned up a
week later in London, drifted to Paris, and
while there had the signal good fortune to
save from annihilation, by an omnibus upon
the asphalt, the Skye terrier of Mrs. Delancey Griffith, a potentate of fashion in
New York. This lady, who wept real tears
upon the restoration of her jewel, could not,
upon further acquaintance with his rescuer,
say enough of her obligation to Mr. Piper.
She murmured something about seeing him
often when they should be back in town,
hinted at tickets to her opera-box, and cups
of tea at her Thursdays, and finally crystal-
lized into an invitation to him to a Christ-

mas party which she had promised to chap-
erone for her brother, at his country place on
the Sound.   The latter suggestion was to Mr.
Clendenning Piper like the vision of a Victoria Cross to an English soldier of the line.
He knew that the hospitalities of the
brother in question, Mr. Peter Percival, were
mentioned in the society columns of the
newspapers as courted by the exclusive
world.   He knew of Mr. Peter Percival himself as a man of many clubs, well-born, well-
placed, and rich ; a bachelor on the shady
side of fifty, for whom nets matrimonial had
long been vainly spread ; given to rallying
about him choice gatherings of people, and
setting before them something original in
his programme for the day or week.   But,
luckily for him, Mr. Piper did not know that
Mrs. Griffith had said, inwardly, before
bestowing on him the eagerly-accepted invitation : " I must do something for this
funny little man who saved my darling

Fussy. Peter's Christmas party will more than pay him up, and I can drop him after that. Peter is so good-natured he won't mind, and, besides, it will set off some horrid new creature he'll be sure to discover and expect me to countenance because she plays on the zither, or recites, or whistles, or dear knows what ! "

By the time Mr. Piper again set foot upon his native shore, many ideas had chased each other through his alleged mind. Upon the threshold of a new existence, as it were a new birth into fashionable life, he had found himself gravely hampered by ties which, viewed in absence and cooler judgment had become quite another thing. As the day drew near to present himself before the lady of his love, he saw, unmistakably, that, as the affianced husband of an insignificant Mrs. Penfold, his chances of becoming a familiar member of Mrs. Griffith's circle would be narrowed hopelessly. He rued the hour in which he had visited Bar Harbor and taken his quarters at the Merry-Go-Round Hotel. Mrs. Penfold's mature age, the lines around her eyes, suspicion of the faint bloom on her cheek, conviction of her want of style, haunted him ceaselessly. . . . . After much mental anguish, he decided upon the course of sending to her address a huge box of American Beauty roses, with a *bonbonnière* of extravagant proportions, and a note regretting that, acting upon the peremptory advice of his physician, he was compelled to pass directly through New York and go South, for a period to which no limit had been set. To justify himself, he arranged to visit the Hygeia Hotel at Old Point Comfort, and remain there until Christmas week.

The invitation given by Mrs. Griffith to Mr. Percival's country house having been duly seconded by that complaisant gentle-

man, we may now behold Mr. Piper on the
eve of realizing his fondest hopes. Fortified
by an English valet and an outfit of English
clothes, he stood ready to join, at their
rendezvous at the Grand Central Station
upon the morrow, the party to which Mrs.
Griffith had decreed that he should be an-
nexed. Fevered with excitement, he spent
the last evening at the play, somewhere, and
on returning to his rooms, found awaiting
him a bombshell in the shape of a communication running thus :

" Mrs. Delancey Griffith's compliments to
Mr. Piper, and regrets that owing to circumstances over which she has no control
the party projected for to-morrow is indefi-
nitely postponed. As Mrs. Griffith is immediately leaving town, she will also be
debarred from receiving her friends on
Thursdays, as proposed."

"What on earth have they heard against
me ?" asked Mr. Piper, wiping the cold

sweat of misery from his haggard brow. "Can it be the newspapers have been publishing something about my engagement to that hanged little widow?"

He passed a sleepless night, and next morning read in the journals served to him with his coffee, announcements of the surprising marriage of the great Mr. Peter Percival with a Mrs. Agnes Blanche Penfold, unknown in the smart set, but said to be a widow encountered by the magnate on a steamer coming from England a few months back. The wedding, occurring at a quiet uptown church the day before, had not been previously announced to Mr. Percival's family, and was now a subject of lively comment in clubs and drawing rooms.

"So that was her game, the little serpent!" spluttered Mr. Piper in a rage; "she wanted to hold on to me for fear of not landing him!"—a mixture of metaphors which, interspersed with language not fitting to record, may be pardoned our hero at this point.

Mr. and Mrs. Peter Percival traveled for some months, and by the time they were ready to reopen the family mansion in New York, so many more startling *dénouements* had been reached in society that they had almost ceased to be discussed. Mrs. Percival, indeed, soon conquered all prejudices, save those of her sister-in-law, Mrs. Delancey Griffith. She makes quite a model great lady, and dispenses her bounties to the fashionable world with a tactful and not too lavish hand. Mr. Piper, who is of a forgiving nature, left his card at the Percivals' soon after her installation in New York; but as he was not included in the invitation to her first general crush, and was hopelessly cut by her in the lobby of the Opera House soon after, he is, at last accounts, on the lookout for some other loophole by which to get into our best society. Neither he nor the late Mrs. Penfold has since favored Bar Harbor with a visit.

JENNY,
THE DÉBUTANTE

ONE fine day in spring, a rattling *fiacre*, driven by a red-nosed, red-waistcoated, and quarrelsome old coachman, pulled up with a jerk before the door of the " Ladies of the Sacred Heart," in a quiet boulevard of Paris.

Out of this equipage, stopping on the sidewalk to pick the straws from her respectable black-worsted ankles, stepped a stout woman with beetling brows that met over a hooked nose.

She wore a black stuff frock and red striped jacket with a clean fluted cap, a costume that indicates her class. She was, in fact, the *bonne*, or maid-of-all-work, sent by Mrs. Platt to accompany that lady's two young daughters back from their convent boarding-school to the fifth-floor apartment in the Rue Vernet that served them as a home.

Annette, at ordinary times so fierce and bustling, had like a true Frenchwoman made ready for her outing by putting on a sort of holiday face. She even exchanged grim jokes with the *cocher* as that functionary, whipping from underneath an oil-skin petticoat around his box a black bottle and a piece of cheese wrapped in a copy of *Le Petit Journal*, with a yard or so of bread, settled himself for a comfortable lunch.

Upon this spectacle the eyes of the two girls rested, when they came out of the convent, the great doors of the best home they had ever known clanging behind them sharply.

" So this is your fairy chariot, Jenny, you little goose ? " Estelle said scornfully.

Jenny could not answer. As they turned the corner of the street she leaned out to look her last at the familiar walls of the beloved Sacred Heart. For the remainder of the drive her little cotton pocket-handkerchief was saturated with very honest tears.

"Do stop crying, Jenny," said her sister. "For my part, bad as it is, I am thankful for any change from that poky place. It was perfectly ridiculous of mamma to keep us there so long."

At Rue Vernet, leaving Annette and the driver to indulge in the usual wrangle over the fare and drink-money, the girls ran with light footsteps up four long flights of stairs. The door was opened for them by their mother, dressed in a tumbled tea-gown of blue china-silk, trimmed with an abundance of not over-clean lace. Mrs. Platt's face looked pinched and tired, under the forest of blond curls she wore when not adorned with crimping pins.

"My dear," said this lady, kissing Estelle on either cheek, then holding her off for a survey, "you really surpass my hopes. One can never tell how a complexion will clear up. Yes, you may go directly into the salon, my child. A friend of mine, Monsieur de Patras, has come to breakfast."

"Mamma!" said an appealing voice.

"O Jenny! is that you, child? And that's the cashmere? How badly it has worn! I declare you're browner than before! The very image of your father's people! Go into my bedroom—or no, you'd better help Annette. Do keep her in a good humor and coax her to make an omelette with jam. I'm sure that woman's temper will bring me to my grave."

Jenny dressed the salad, arranged a few grapes and pears, tidied the scantily served table, and at last, to soothe the now raging Annette, undertook to make the coffee, and to watch the omelette. She heard Estelle singing, at the little cracked piano, a song from the " Noces de Jeannette " they had both learned at the convent :

Cours, mon aiguille, dans la laine.

And afterward the approving voice of Monsieur de Patras, crying "Brava, brava !" She caught a glimpse of that gentleman sitting on a little sofa nursing his hat and stick, and his moustachios amused her mightily.

By the time Jenny found an opportunity to eat her own scrappy midday meal, Estelle and her mamma had gone off to drive in the Bois de Boulogne, in Monsieur de Patras's carriage.

" And you will dine afterward with me at the restaurateur's, *chère Madame ?* " the Baron had said, in setting out. " Perhaps it will amuse Mademoiselle to visit the *spectacle* at the Châtelet, this evening."

" You are too good, Monsieur, to my little

convent-bred girl," madame had answered, fluttering with satisfaction. "Think what it has been to me to be separated from this dear angel;" at which moment Annette, putting her blunt head in at the door, had summoned her mistress to know what she expected to have for dinner, now that the chops had been sacrificed to the "*second déjeuner*."

"How dare you interrupt me?" said the lady in a sharp whisper. "Idiot! cook anything you have. Mademoiselle and I do not return till after the *spectacle* to-night."

Poor little Jenny, who would have given her eyes to see the old story of Cinderella acted with a hundred tricks of stagecraft about which all Paris had been talking latterly, was forgotten. Luckily, the girls in the convent school, except those who, when at home for the holidays, were taken by their guardians to see an occasional fairy piece, knew very little about theatrical delights. Jenny, too, was accustomed

through long habit to give up to Estelle ;
and, in unpacking their boxes and practicing
a while on the piano, the afternoon was
passed not unpleasantly. Old Annette,
mollified by her helpfulness, managed to
prepare for her tea a delicious dish of toasted
rusk, with apples spiced and roasted and a
tiny pot of cream.

"For with that *charcutier* at the corner,
insisting as he does on being paid, *ma foi*,"
the woman said, "another scrap of meat
this day is not a thing to think of."

The first day of Jenny's life at home was
a sample of those that followed. She used
often to think longingly of the merry companionship of the girls at the *Sacré Cœur*.
She missed more than she could say the
gentle sympathy of Sister Geneviève, the
nun who had been "faither an' mither an'
a'," to the two young Americans growing up
in her charge.

For Mrs. Platt, who had been a widow
ever since Jenny's babyhood, had long ago
fallen in with the vagrant, hand-to-mouth
style of living pursued by a certain number
of her country people in Europe. It had
been to her a great convenience to tuck
away Estelle and Jenny in the safe precincts
of the convent school while she traveled
about in the wake of a floating colony of
idle people, who are seen at Paris, Hom-
burg, Rome, Nice, etc., in turn.

But Estelle and Jenny, heretofore spoken
of as " my darling little girls," had perse-
vered in a habit healthy girls have—of growing and budding and putting out all manner
of fresh charms and graces, until Sister
Geneviève had felt obliged to inform their
mother it was time to take them home " for
good."

Poor Mrs. Platt was at first really over-
whelmed. How could her scant supply of
ready money be made to cover the expenses

of three who must share and share alike?
Estelle, with her beautiful coloring and
stylish figure, might indeed help to reflect
credit on the widow ; but Jenny—Jenny,
little, brown, bright-eyed, like a robin on
a twig—who could do anything with such
as Jenny?

As the May days passed away, and all of
Paris—beautiful, bewildering, blossoming,
laughing Paris in spring garb—poured out
upon the streets and parks and drives and
boulevards, Mrs. Platt and Estelle were continually abroad. To provide both of them
with the wonderful toilets in which they
appeared in public, the little day-dress-
maker could never have sewed fast enough,
unless Jenny's fingers had been there to
help. Jenny sewed long seams, hemmed
ruffles, tied bows and, when Estelle was
attired for conquest, stood back to admire the lovely vision she had helped to
create. For Estelle, aided by her mother's

taste in dress, was beautiful, undoubtedly. Many people of Mrs. Platt's acquaintance, who for some time past had taken little notice of the widow, left cards and renewed their invitations, in consideration of the new attraction the Rue Vernet now offered.

There was, however, one person who had never been brought to recognize the social claims of Mrs. Platt, and that was her countrywoman, Mrs. Noble of New York, who with her young family occupied the best apartment of the house in the Rue Vernet. It was too exasperating, the widow thought, to have everybody taking for granted that she knew her "charming compatriot, the distinguished Madame Noble."

In spite of many opportunities of which she might well have taken advantage, Mrs. Noble had remained blind and deaf to the existence of Mrs. Platt. Every day, coming and going, it was the widow's lot to see

the Nobles' carriage, drawn by those famous
American horses, standing in the courtyard; to see Mrs. Noble with her son or
daughter get into it and drive away, without a glance in her direction. The wealth,
the ease, the assured position of the Nobles,
were what the foolish woman envied ; not
the good breeding, the family union, the
simplicity of dress and manner that marked
her neighbors *au premier.*

Little Jenny, tripping up and down the
stairs, unnoticed, to save Annette's old
bones in household errands, found herself too, one day, looking after the Nobles'
carriage as it drove away from the courtyard, with a sort of yearning in her heart.
She had heard an interchange of loving
banter between the mother and her children,
and the contrast between that and her own
domestic atmosphere went through her with
a pang.

Early in June came invitations, for which

Mrs. Platt had plotted and planned with persistence worthy of a better cause, to a fête at the *hôtel* of one of the ministers of government; a ball, with dancing in a tent to be pitched in the middle of an illuminated garden. Monsieur de Patras had brought the two rose-colored tickets that were to admit Estelle and her mamma into this dazzling scene.

New dresses, fresh in every particular, with the exception, perhaps, of the makeshift by which madame's old pink silk might be made to serve under a new pink gauze for mademoiselle, were absolutely necessary. The little dressmaker, Jenny, madame, and Estelle (who directed but did not sew) met together daily in important conclave. The sitting room fairly overflowed with flounces and furbelows and snippings of tulle and silk and ribbon. Jenny, as much excited as if she herself were to be the happy wearer of the robe now nearly finished, had sewed until she began to feel a chronic headache.

"There is one thing I forgot to tell you, Estelle," said excited Mrs. Platt on the morning of the fête ; "I am told that the Nobles will certainly be there, and a friend has promised to introduce us to them without fail. Really, my dear, you are looking pale to-day. Come out with me for a walk, and if I can possibly afford it I will bargain with the florist to let you have a bouquet for to-night that will be worth the carrying."

"May I go for a walk in the Parc Monceaux, mamma?" asked Jenny. "Marie and I can't both sew at once on your skirt, and I have been feeling rather dizzy."

"Yes, go," answered the mother shortly. "The Parc Monceaux is so given up to nursery maids and children you can walk there alone. Besides, nobody would be likely to notice *you*, I think!" she ended, with a little slighting laugh.

Jenny had often before found her solitary way to the pretty little park in the heart of the great bustling city near their home. In her plain frock, with her threadbare gloves, the girl could glide about unobserved, like the modest little working woman that she was.

Sometimes a child at play would stop to talk to her, and dogs scampering away from their owners would frisk and lick her hand when she accosted them. The birds knew her and her pocket full of crumbs; but with these exceptions Jenny had for the most part the companionship of only her cheerful thoughts.

For I defy anyone who has youth and strength and the future stretching far ahead to be doleful in such an atmosphere as that of an early summer's day in Paris. The sparkle of sunshine, the green of grass and trees, the play of fountains and the brilliant show of flowers and, over all, such a stir and murmuring of re-awakened nature, enjoyed by throngs of pleasant-spoken people, are quite irresistible.

Jenny made no attempt to resist it. She walked more rapidly, she hummed, she skipped. Turning into a shady avenue of horse-chestnuts, she found herself alone. A little Scotch terrier, gamboling without his leash, ran with her. When tired of racing him she stopped by a fountain, and from the leaves of a broken bough of horse-chestnut made for herself a cup, and stooped to drink.

" Here, Rags ! here, Rags ! " said a pleasant voice, calling the little dog. Jenny looked up, and saw on a bench near by, their neighbor, Mrs. Noble.

" Oh ! Rags is such a darling little fellow," she exclaimed ; " I hope you do not mind my racing him."

" Rags is a wise little fellow," said his mistress, smiling. " He knows how to

choose his comrades for a game. Of course
he gets tired sometimes of following my
sober steps, and my own poor girl isn't
strong enough to run with him. See here,
my child, I have a fancy to taste water from
a leaf-cup like the one you threw away;
won't you make another one for me?"

Jenny made the cup, and, after drinking,
Mrs. Noble sighed. " It was on my father's
farm in Massachusetts—I don't like to
think how many years ago—that I quaffed
my last draught from such a sylvan goblet.
It was for old associations' sake I asked
you."

"Then you can tell me about America," cried Jenny, kindling. "My father,
too, I think lived in Massachusetts as a boy.
I don't know anything about my own
country except what the geographies tell
us—and at a French convent that's not
much."

Unconsciously she had seated herself at

the other end of Mrs. Noble's bench. She took her hat off, and the heat making her hair curl into rings of golden brown around her temples, deepened the color in her cheeks. Jenny looked—yes, it is actually true—so pretty, that the lady of the fountain smiled admiringly. Mrs. Noble, interested in the subject as in her listener, talked long and pleasantly.

When, in the course of their conversation, she found out that Jenny was the child of the Mrs. Platt who lived *au cinquième* in the Rue Vernet, an expression Jenny could hardly understand came into her mild eyes.

" I do not know your mother," she said, after a moment's pause. " But, my dear, if you think she will not mind, it would give me the greatest pleasure to take you with us this evening to hear Madame Galli-Marié sing the part of *Mignon* at the Opéra-Comique."

12

"*I*—oh!" Jenny drew a long breath of pleasure. "I have never heard an opera. The Sisters took us to a Mass at St. Eustache one day; we heard the 'Stabat Mater.' Oh! how thrilling it all was. There was a man's voice—he came from the Pope's choir, they said; it was like an angel's trumpet! Oh! do you believe mamma will let me?" she concluded, in a burst of joyful incoherence.

"I believe she will," said Mrs. Noble smiling.

It was all astonishing, Jenny thought. There were mamma and Estelle lying on their beds, trying to get a little sleep, they said, before dressing for the ball. (Mamma was in a queer kind of humor, half pleased, half snappish!) There was little Marie, the sewing-girl, lingering beyond her time to fasten Jenny's one white frock, the muslin Sister Geneviève had ordered for their school exhibition the year before. Marie's deft fingers tied her white silk sash in a truly Parisian bow behind the slender waist, and when all was finished stood back to inform Jenny that she was *vraiment très bien;* not beautiful like Mademoiselle Estelle, but *comme il faut!* There was Annette, in a red camisole and spotless cap, waiting to escort her down the stairs and deliver her up in state to Mrs. Noble's keeping! Surely, it could not be true. Surely, little Jenny must awake and find it but a dream.

Jenny had never seen anything like the elegance and comfort of her new friend's quarters. When the doors opened, and she was ushered into the large drawing room filled with luxurious furniture and hangings, with blooming plants everywhere, and softly-shaded lamps, with abundant books and work-tables, and an open grand piano, behind which sat a young girl playing one

of Chopin's waltzes, she felt absolutely overcome with fear.

But there, in a deep armchair, holding
out her hand and gently greeting her little
visitor, was the lady of the fountain. Behind Mrs. Noble stood her tall son, George,
and Helen came forward from the piano.

"See, children," said Mrs. Noble, when
they rose to go in to dinner presently,
"did I not tell you truly? Jenny has
just the turn of the head, the trick of
looking up when spoken to. I am speaking of my married daughter in New York,
my dear; you reminded me of Grace the
moment I laid eyes on you."

"And you must expect to be spoiled
outrageously in consequence," said Helen.
"Mamma can never forgive my brother-in-
law for carrying off her eldest."

The dinner was pleasant, and uncon-
strained beyond anything in Jenny's previ-
ous experience. When the carriage was an-

nounced to take the ladies to the opera, Mrs.
Noble gave to each of the girls a bunch of
deep-red roses and, drawing Jenny aside
to her own room, put something in her
hand.

"There, my dear, is a little trinket to
wear on that velvet at your throat—a mere
trifle of a thing, but I found it in my jewel-
box, and it will remind you of our meeting
at the fountain."

Eagerly Jenny opened the little velvet
box to find a pendant resembling a leaf,
made of green enamel, on which lay a pearl
and two tiny diamonds. Needless to tell of
her rapture when Helen slipped the pretty
ornament—her very, very first!—upon the
velvet round her neck.

Jenny went to bed that night as happy
as a queen. She was up next morning and
about her work, long before it was time to
carry mamma's and Estelle's chocolate into
their bedrooms. From her sister she re-

ceived no greeting, but Mrs. Platt plied her with a hundred questions.

" Humph ! " said that lady, when she had heard a full account of Jenny's evening of pure bliss. " A dinner—the opera—roses—pearls and diamonds ! Upon my word, Miss, you are prettily set up. I must say it was a thousand pities you got that slice of luck, instead of poor Estelle. Was there ever anything so provoking as my missing Mrs. Noble's call, when she came yesterday to leave the note asking if you might go with her ? However, Estelle and I will make it a point to return the visit this afternoon. Mrs. Noble ought to see Estelle."

" I hope your ball was lovely," ventured Jenny in return.

"Well, the crowd was awful. I lost my fan, and Estelle's gown was torn nearly in two. There was not much chance for dancing, and we walked around with that stupid old Patras until our feet ached. I think it very strange, Jenny, that the Nobles were not there. I thought they would be sure to look in after they left you at home."

"I heard Mrs. Noble say that she did not approve of taking a girl so young as Helen to those semi-public balls, and that she herself never went into a crush," said Jenny; a remark that had the immediate effect of making her mother scold her for impertinence until the poor girl burst into tears, and hurried from the room.

Spite of its auspicious beginning, the acquaintance between the families of Platt and Noble did not appear to flourish. Mrs. Noble was from home when Mrs. Platt called on the afternoon following the ball. Maneuver as she might, Mrs. Platt could find no way of introducing her darling Estelle to such important notice.

"I have it," said Mrs. Platt, coming in to her eldest daughter's room; "Mrs. Noble has asked Jenny to meet her in the park

for a walk this morning.   It is easy enough
for me to keep that tiresome little Jenny
in.   There is always work enough for her
to do at home.   Do you dress yourself,
Estelle, in that *écru pongee* with the
embroidered parasol to match, and the
knots of poppy-colored ribbon. You are
sweet in that. Annette shall walk with
you, and you can introduce yourself to Mrs.
Noble by saying you came to bring Jenny's
apologies.   Come, don't sulk, my darling ;
you know Mrs. Noble can do *everything*
for you if she only takes the fancy."

It was with no very good grace, however,
that Estelle followed these directions. When
she reached the park, she ordered Annette
to sit down upon a bench, which the overworked old woman was glad enough to do.

Strolling up and down the avenue leading
to the fountain, Estelle's heart was filled
with weariness and unsatisfied longing. She
resented her mother for the schemes of

which she was beginning to heartily tire, she resented Jenny's gleam of good fortune. Everything seemed jaundiced in her sight.

No sign yet of Jenny's good Fairy of the Fountain. In her place, an elderly English maid was crocheting on a bench, a small dog was careering wildly around the gravel walk. A light puff of wind blew Estelle's parasol from her hand. The fall detached a bow of poppy-colored ribbon which blew over upon the grass. In a moment the little dog was after it. Estelle called to him angrily, but the mischievous little fellow ran the faster with his prize. By the time she came up with him, he had chewed the ribbon into a shapeless mass.

The angry blood rushed into Estelle's face. With the stick of her parasol she beat the dog so fiercely that he clamored with pain. She did not see or care who looked at her. A moment later, a girl, whom she did not at first recognize as Helen Noble, had picked up the terrier and clasped it to her breast.

"You are a wicked, cruel person!" cried Helen, confronting Estelle with a degree of energy born of her righteous indignation. "I know you, and I would not speak to you if it were not for my poor Rags. I believe you have half killed him."

"I wish I had killed him," returned Estelle angrily.

"Come, Miss Noble, this is no company for you," said the prim maid, who had been crocheting on the bench. "I wonder what Mrs. Noble will say when she hears the way her pet has been a-treated? One thing's certain—she'll find out fine feathers don't make fine birds, I'm thinking," and she darted a resentful glance at Estelle's finery.

Estelle's cowardly heart began to beat with quite a new sensation. How came it that she had not known Helen Noble? This

was the end, then, of all the wiles and
schemes. While trying to think how she
could smooth the matter over, she found
herself alone. The occasional outcries of
poor little wounded Rags, as he was borne
away, on the gravel at her feet a crushed
and soiled knot of ribbon on which a toad
was sitting, were all that remained to tell
the tale of her defeat!

By midsummer, Paris was deserted by the
fashionable world, and Mrs. Platt, following
the example of her richer friends, betook
herself, her older daughter, and several
trunks full of made-over furbelows, to various places of resort.

Jenny tried bravely to bear up against
the solitude of the long hot days, but the
strain was terrible. Many a time did her
thoughts turn to the alleys of the convent garden, and to Sister Geneviève ; but
Paris lay between them and she had no

money to pay cab-fare, and dared not go on foot. Of the Nobles, she knew only that they had set out on a long journey; to Norway, she had heard. Since the encounter with Estelle at the fountain, Mrs. Platt, in a fury at the insult, as she chose to call it, directed to her child, had refused to let Jenny accept any farther notice from the family. Jenny never received the kind note written by Mrs. Noble on leaving Paris, bidding the girl keep a brave heart and not forget those, who would one day find her out again. "Such impudence!" Mrs. Platt had remarked, waylaying the billet, and taking care that it did not reach the little girl, who was at that moment crying her eyes out on her cot because she believed her friends had gone away offended beyond recall.

And at last, one morning, Annette, going into Jenny's bedroom, found her complaining of a bad sore throat, with pains unlike any she had known before laying hold of all her

limbs. Annette had not money wherewith
to pay a doctor, and the *concierge*, summoned into council, procured a physician
from an infirmary, who straightway pronounced the disease to be diphtheria.

It is an old saying that Paris is a capital
place to laugh and be merry in, but a poor
one in which to sorrow, to suffer, or to die.
The *concierge*, hearing the doctor's decree,
consulted *M. le Propriétaire*, who with scant
preparation (having, indeed, but little regard
for a family of tenants whose rent was already overdue) bundled Miss Jenny and her
belongings off to a hospital.

"Sister Geneviève! Oh! let me have
Sister Geneviève!" repeated the girl incessantly, as delirium set in.

Jenny always said she went to sleep in the
ward of a common hospital, and woke up
in Paradise. What her eyes really opened
upon, when fever left them, was a little

chamber with walls tinted a cool green, a wide window draped with dimity, through which she could see a mass of waving tree-tops under a summer sky. Street sounds, mellowed by distance, came to her not unpleasantly. The few articles of furniture in the room were exquisitely clean and neat. She saw a vase of honeysuckle on the dressing-stand, and smelt its delicious odor. Then she closed her eyes again and on next awaking, refreshed, and anxious to ask questions, there, at her elbow, with a cup of iced bouillon, was dear Sister Geneviève.

Before Jenny had a chance to express her satisfaction at the sight, the door opened to admit a lady in wrap and bonnet; none other than Mrs. Noble, who, journeying back to Paris with her son in answer to a call on business from her banker, had reached the Rue Vernet to hear from the *concierge* of Jenny's removal to the hospital.

A very ill person does not trouble to know where comforts come from. Jenny did not hear, until nearly well again, how it was Mrs. Noble, who had removed her to a private room of an English hospital of which she happened to be lady-patroness; how Sister Geneviève, summoned to take the invalid in charge, had nursed her tenderly through a perilous attack; how Mrs. Noble, refusing to leave Paris again until Jenny's convalescence was established, came every day for news of her.

Letters written to inform Mrs. Platt of these events miscarried and, no answer to them coming, Mrs. Noble took the affair in her own hands. The latter part of a summer opening so dismally for Jenny was spent with her dearest friend in one of the loveliest spots of the High Pyrenees.

When Mrs. Platt did hear of these occurrences, she was divided between relief and anger. But her marriage with M. de Patras occurring just then, she was inclined to be forgiving. This marriage secured a home for Estelle and herself, but about Jenny there was the usual difficulty. The Baron, who had no great fortune, did not welcome so large a family.

In this emergency, Jenny took heart to confide to her mother an offer George Noble had made, to transfer the little waif entirely into his own keeping, to return with him as his wife to America, where he was to find employment in the management of the paternal estates.

"Jenny! Why, Jenny!" said the new Mme. de Patras, "it's hardly possible Mrs. Noble should—it's just like a fairy-tale—but if she *is* willing to let George marry you, there's not a *débutante* in the American colony this year that's made her market half as well as you. I always thought you took after me rather than your father—he, poor man, had no foresight, no management—

he was exactly like Estelle. Come here,
and kiss me, you dear little brown mouse!"

" Everything has a moral, if you can only
find it," says the sprightly Duchess in " Al-
ice in Wonderland "; and this is mine—*naïf*
and time-worn, but distinctly " up to date":
" Kind words are as precious as pearls and
diamonds, and as sweet as roses. Cross,
unkind words are as bad as toads and
vipers."

WIFE'S LOVE.

[A Folk Tale told to a party of American tourists in Norway. Old Clemens, the guide, speaks.]

SUCH a pretty girl was Aslog, daughter of a great Norwegian chieftain of the olden time. White and soft was her skin as the swan's-down of her Sunday cap and mantle. Red roses bloomed in her cheeks, a kind smile hovered around her little mouth, and her blue eyes looked frank and fearless upon the world about her. Lonely enough was Aslog's bit of this big world, and at times a chill, drear spot ; but at times again full of radiant color, and of the chatter of nesting ducks and the dash of waterfalls. Her father's house was like the eyrie of a wild bird, built in the cleft of frowning rocks above the rude North Sea. Happy? Aye, that was she; as happy as the day is long in Norway, until she fell in love with Orm, one of the young fellows employed by the chief, her father, to guard his herds, to hunt and fish for him, and to fight his battles whenever called upon. How this falling in love came about I know not. Who knows why the wind blows, why birds seek their mates, why the snowdrop bursts its sheath and blooms into a flower? Aslog saw Orm, and her heart went into his keeping forevermore. As for Orm, he would have died to save her little finger from a scratch; at least he said so, and lovers always tell the truth.

When Orm asked Aslog's father for her hand there was a dreadful scene. The old man stormed at the young people, shut Aslog up in her bower, drove Orm off the premises in short order. Didn't Orm know, didn't everybody know that the Lady As-

log was soon to marry her cousin, the great
sea-captain, who was just then coming home
from a cruise in which he had burnt and de-
spoiled the ships of many enemies? Not
until grass grew down and streams ran backward should this fitting match be broken!
No! There was an end of it!

Alsog, through her tears, caught a glimpse
of her tall young lover standing pale but
resolute before the angry chief. As her
maidens hustled her away, she managed to
give Orm one sweet look that warmed his
heart.

A month later, the wedding of Aslog
and her cousin was announced to take place
upon the morrow. That night, through
wind and storm, the lovers fled to the dwelling of the old priest who had baptized the
girl, and who could refuse her nothing. He
warmed them, gave them wine and food,
and in the presence of his ancient serving

maid and man made them husband and wife.

"Not for your sake only, my nestling," the old priest said, "but for your mother's, who, in dying, asked me to save you from a fate like hers—a marriage without love. Orm have I known from boyhood; he is brave and true, and worthy even of you. Go now, and may Heaven keep you from all harm."

That *was* a wedding journey! Orm had but one present for his bride, a cloak of seal-skin, trophy of his hunts. The wedding ring was a beauty, of beaten gold, like serpents twisted with jewels for their scales! The young couple had to climb in the darkness up a steep, rocky pathway, where a goat would have hard work to keep his footing, let alone a Christian. Orm knew the track, since he was the boldest hunter in the old chief's band; and when Aslog trembled overmuch he took her in his arms and strode along the verge of the precipice, and laughed and talked to cheer her.

Ere long they reached the home he had secretly made ready for her—a deep, dry cavern, all glittering inside, with chairs and couches spread with skins and birds' plumage. There were bowls and cups beautifully shaped from wood; for Orm was a rare hand to carve. There was a cask of mead; there were strings of dried fish, and game and eggs in plenty. Oh, no fear of starving, or of freezing either; and as the fire they kindled sent up its blue smoke into the cavern's chimney, Aslog's pale cheeks reddened with returning warmth.

"To think you had to carry all this up that terrible pathway, Orm!" she said, exulting in his strength and daring. And Orm said the last load he had carried was the lightest.

For some time the runaways kept close watch on the valley below; but, although they could plainly see the search parties sent out for them, nobody found out their retreat; and so the winter wore away. Orm hunted, while Aslog kept up the fire, cooked, broidered a little (for she had brought a needle and some stuffs), and tried not to feel lonely when her man was away from her side. But it wouldn't have been natural for the poor child to forget her home. She used to picture the great hall, the fire snapping, the maidens spinning, the songs sung by her father's minstrels, the music made upon golden harps.

But this was only when Orm was belated. When he came in, strong and loving, nothing seemed to make much difference to Aslog. One day he brought with him a broken-winged eaglet for her to tame; and after that Aslog had company while he was gone.

Spring came. The huge waterfall, dashing down the heights hard by, softened its roar, the ice melted, the valley put on its green.

" Now I have nothing more to ask," cried the happy Aslog ; but one day Orm ran in breathless, to say that he had seen her cousin, the sea-captain, with a band of followers, spying out the path by which the lovers had escaped.

" Now must we fly, my darling," he added ; " for I ventured near enough to hear them talking, and to-morrow they are determined to find a way to us. It is the fault of the bow which I let fall over the cliff, last week, which they found and knew to be mine."

That evening the lovers crept down to the shore, where Orm had hidden a boat in case of an alarm. They set sail upon a dark and stormy sea, and for three days the tempest raged, blinding Orm, till he knew not

his right hand from the left. It seemed to
him that they were nearing shore, but that
a mighty blast of wind was blowing them
back from it. At last his strong arm grew
weak, and he could no longer grasp the rud-
der. Aslog, seeing their peril, uttered a
fervent prayer. At once the wind ceased,
and the boat drifted quietly into a little
bay, where green grass grew close to a beach
of sparkling sand. Astonished and delighted, Orm anchored the boat. He
looked about him and saw that they had
reached an island, apparently deserted.

Two odd things they beheld not far
ahead of them. One was a huge Stone Man
sitting, like a monument. The other a
cone-shaped hill of grass soft as green
velvet, with smoke issuing from a chimney at the top, and with a closed door, to
which led up a path of glittering pink
shells.

Shipwrecked people are not easily scared

by what they first see on *terra firma*, and the
husband and wife took heart to pass by the
Stone Man, follow up the shell walk and
knock at the hill door. No answer; but the
door slowly swung open, and there, within,
they espied a dainty, shining hall, containing, at one end, a single large armchair, or
throne, and, all about it, little stools and
easy-chairs of silver, with not a soul to sit in
them ! The rest of the Hill House was in
order for housekeeping—fires burning, white
beds spread, a pot bubbling on the hearth,
delicious smells coming out of it. Tables,
cupboards with silver plates and spoons,
chairs, everything ! Even a flagon of wine,
with beakers, on the shelf.

Starving and athirst, they could not wait
the return of the owner of this delightful
spot. Orm gave food to his wife, then a
draught of wine, after which he, too, ate and
drank. At once, a deep sleep fell upon the
two, and they felt invisible hands bearing

them and laying them on beds of eider down.

How long they slept they knew not. On awaking, they found a tall, stately woman sitting in an armchair by the fire. As she arose, her great height and noble bearing convinced the pair that they were in the presence of a giantess, a race then almost vanished out of Norway.

"Fear not," she said kindly. "I am the Giantess Gurn, and this is a country place of mine, where I sometimes come to pass a week or two. Our race is at enmity with yours, and so when I saw your boat approaching my island, I amused myself by standing on the cliff, and blowing you out with my breath to sea again. But the prayer you uttered conquered me, and thus you drifted in unharmed. When I saw that you were a young wife and husband, so loving and so tender, my heart melted, and I let you have the food and rest you needed."

Orm and his Aslog kissed the hands of the gentle giantess in silence, offering to take their leave. But the Lady of the Hill bade them tarry; and when next she spoke tears came in her eyes.

"Never shall it be told that I failed to befriend two loving hearts that beat as one," she said. "Look out of the door and see yonder stone image sitting there, and know that it is none other than my husband, whom I cherished tenderly. Condemned to remain in that shape by the magic of an enemy more powerful than we, once a year I have power to bring my dear lord to life again by sacrificing a hundred years of my own existence. Gladly, gladly are they given; for what is life to me without him? Soon my span will be over, and I shall go to take my place beside him. Answer me not, for mortals may not hold familiar converse with giants of a grand old race like ours; but heed. Your story I have ascertained,

and I feel for you. Homeless outcasts as
you are, this house may shelter you until I
come again next Yule, and longer if you
obey my orders. On Christmas Eve you
must go up into the loft and remain there
in hiding until dawn, when we depart.
Strange ceremonies do we hold then, when
our subjects pay their homage to my lord
and me. Should mortal eye behold us at
our revels, and it were known that I permitted this breach of our laws, you and
yours would be punished cruelly, while I
would lose another hundred years of my
existence upon earth."

Orm and Aslog strove to speak, but their
tongues clove to the roofs of their mouths,
as if in some weird dream. They could
only kneel and thank their benefactress in
dumb show. Then, to their astonishment,
they saw the lady, grown taller and more
majestic, go down the path to the water,
stoop and kiss the Stone Man as she passed,

and, wading deliberately out into the sea, vanish from their sight beneath the foam crest of a mighty wave.

Affairs prospered with Orm and Aslog after the strange interview, and shortly before Christmas they had a son, so strong and beautiful no baby ever equaled him. As Christmas approached, Aslog made ready the Hill House for the festival, dusting and scrubbing until no speck was left. On the appointed night they took the baby and climbed up into the loft. The sea roared, the wind howled, there was a strange tremor in the air. From the chinks of the roof, they could see the wide expanse of water around their rock-bound home wrinkled with seething waves, over which danced, dipped, and courtesied lights, red, blue, violet, and orange, drawing ever nearer to the island. After these lights came together and formed in a long procession to march up to the house, they gathered

around the figure of the Stone Man, and
stood still. Then was heard the sound as
of the swoop of mighty swan's wings
through the air. A mighty, mysterious
shape, clad in luminous white, descended
upon the Island, and cast a cloud of silver
brightness around the Stone Man. Shouts
arose, hoarse and shrill, as if from numbers
of dwarf throats. Aslog, frightened out
of her wits, threw her arms around Orm's
neck and clung to him in silence. The
baby, sucking his thumb, slept unconscious
of the turmoil.

And now the procession of light-bearers
drew near the house, the Stone Man walking
with a tread that shook the earth, beside
Gurn, who wore a gown like hoarfrost, with
a crown of sparkling diamonds. The
torches, borne by hundreds of little elves,
made the scene as distinct as if it were
broad day; but when once the revelers
had crossed the Hill House threshold

Orm and Aslog dared no longer look at them, even though a crevice in the loft floor presented itself provokingly close to Aslog's very feet.

Laughter, talk, odors of delicious food and drink floated up to the married pair, who still stood motionless, wreathed in each other's arms. Then, alas! began the tuning of tiny harps and fiddles, at the first sounds of which the mortals started, as if at an electric shock.

"I did not bargain for elf-music," Orm said, palpitating, his breath beginning to come quicker.

"Oh! husband, husband!" cried Aslog, panting, as the first silver strain rang out. Music that sent sweet madness coursing like quicksilver in the listeners' blood. Music that wooed sea-monsters from the deep, sea-birds from the air, to gather by hundreds round the island. What mere mortal could withstand it?

14

"Heaven send they play not the Elf-King's Merry Round," cried the terrified Orm, seeing that his full strength could with difficulty restrain the struggles of his wife; "for when that's played, all who hear must dance to it or die."

With reeling brain, with twitching hands and feet, Aslog listened; and when suddenly the measure changed to one of quicker time, dangerously sweet, like tinkling flower bells mixed with shattered bird notes, she gave one great, convulsive gasp, and, wrenching herself from her husband's arms, darted down the ladder, and danced into the middle of the room below.

Orm heard an exclamation of dismay in gentle Gurn's voice, then a mad hurly-burly of groans and cries of rage from the insulted dwarfs.

"Save her! Save my Aslog!" he cried aloud, his feet twitching and stumbling as he stooped over to reach his baby in the cradle. Before he could lift the child into the protection of his arms, the little disturbed creatures below ran with the speed of light up the ladder, snatched the baby and made off with it. Blinded and despairing, Orm staggered after them and stood in the hall below. All was confusion. The torches, swirling together like the figures in a kaleidoscope, were suddenly put out, and in the darkness he felt himself pinched and tugged and beaten by invisible hands.

"Aslog, my own," he cried out with one last effort, and fell, stunned and motionless, upon the floor.

When consciousness returned, he lay alone on the cold hearth. Instantly Orm remembered what had befallen him. Half crazed, he dashed out into the night, calling aloud for Aslog and his baby. No answer but the dash of angry waves upon the cliff. As of old, the Stone Man sat dumb and unsympathizing on his pedestal.

Orm went back, chilled and heart sore, to his forsaken dwelling. It was cold comfort to him to find the floor strewn with fairy relics. There were little glass slippers, with shoe-strings of red ribbon, harps, fiddles, dulcimers, plates, goblets, flagons of pure gold and silver, hammered by elf-hands underground, and set with rarest gems. There was Gurn's mantle fallen across her chair, all woven of eider-down tissue, and broidered thick with silver threads. To possess all—nay half of these—meant riches to a mortal; but what use was wealth to a man who had lost Aslog and her baby?

Time went on. Orm had endured life he knew not how. At Easter-tide, he was again sitting sadly in the room. He had come home from fishing, and, on the way, had plucked a bunch of early blue harebells growing in a cleft of the rocks. "How Aslog would have welcomed them," he said, and with the words a pang came that made him cast the tiny things despairingly away. At that moment the noise of great wings was heard, and a shadow fell across the doorway. It was none other than Gurn, pale, unsmiling, and weaker than of old, who alighted at his side.

"No grudge do I bear you, mortal," she said, in solemn tones. "Your punishment has been great; and before I go hence to join my dear one in his eternal sleep of stone, where to-morrow's rise of sun shall find me, I have asked a last favor of the dwarfs, and they have granted it. At Easter dawn your darlings shall be restored to you. Farewell, remember Gurn!"

Orm's heart gave a mighty bound; he believed that it broke then and there with joy. All grew dark before him. Trying to kiss the hem of his benefactor's garment he fell forward on his face.

Here, in the earliest rays of Easter sunlight, Aslog and her baby came to him. At

the first touch of his wife's hand Orm stirred
from his trance, and opened his eyes upon
her rosy face.   Never had it seemed to him
so fair.

What most astonished Orm, however, was
that, after greeting him tenderly, Aslog set
about her household tasks as if she had
never been away.   Where she had been,
how she came back, she could not say.   We
who know the old trick of fairy kidnappers,
how they always rob their captives of
memory before restoring them to earth, are
not so much inclined to wonder as was our
simple Orm.

Presently the husband and wife left their
baby in the cradle and wandered out into
the gladness of the newborn day.   Oh, sad
and strange sight!   There, beside the Stone
Man, her calm lips smiling peacefully, her
sightless eyes opened full upon the rising
sun, sat the Gentle Giantess, turned, like her
mate, to stone.

Aslog plucked flowers and laid them in her lap. Orm vowed that he would build around the faithful pair a wall so broad and strong that it should stand for ages.

In the course of time a ship, coming to anchor in the bay of Orm's Island, found Aslog and her husband living in peace and happiness. They took this occasion, however, to journey back to their former home, where, by the sale of some of his fairy silverware and trinkets, Orm found himself a rich man, able to beg forgiveness from the father of his wife.

The old chief, they say, warmly urged the young people to remain with him. But the Hill House was their favorite dwelling-place, and there they spent their lives.

Orm's children moved away from the island, as years went on; but if you go to visit the spot to-day you will certainly find there the figures of the Stone Man and his Gentle Giantess.

A HARP UNSTRUNG.

ONE evening in March, George Talbot had gathered in his comfortable old-time dining room a merry company. An invitation to one of his well-appointed bachelor dinners was considered by aspirants to social place in New York a brevet of fashion. On this occasion the party was chaperoned by Mrs. Malbone—large, bland, platitudinous —wearing the famous Malbone necklace under her triple chin. It included the more promising elements of the latest bride, two of the newest beauties, a clever widow, little Mrs. Bob Stryker, from Baltimore— who makes every party go—an English earl, in search of an American "Motor," Regy

Glenham, Langford, of the *Age*, Mrs. Bob's husband, *et al.*, as the lawyers say.

Talbot himself, at the foot of the table, on which the silver candlesticks and India china, cut-glass and thick white damask bespoke the fittings of a generation past, was by all odds the most distinguished figure of the circle. The slim little earl, with his patches of whitish whisker on a pair of continually blushing cheeks, made a poor show of weight and girth and muscle beside his stately host. Talbot resembled the oak of the Western forest rather than the iron-bound elm that has sprung between city paving-stones. And yet, save for his campaigns in the war between the States and the easy journeys here and there around the world of an untrammeled man of means, his life had been spent in New York; most of it in the same house, whither his mother had come as a bride, now five-and-forty years ago.

There had been no Mrs. Talbot to succeed that worthy lady. Worse luck, thought some of the marriageable maidens, in whose eyes the quiet dwelling in the conservative quarter of the eastern part of the town—the broad, red-brick, " English-basement" house with its old furniture, old books and pictures, customs and servants, and the not particularly young master—had an attraction hard to rival.

For it, and for him, did they and their mammas cheerfully forsake the brown-stone haunts of the elect uptown, where night by night are spread banquets of Lucullus, each so patterned after the other that the givers of the feasts alone accentuate the difference between them.

" The truth is," said lively Mrs. Bob to her neighbor, Regy Glenham, as she leaned across him to help herself to salted almonds, " you New York people are getting tired of your everlasting straining after style. You aren't quite certain *what* style, don't you know? If there were only a fixed law, it would be such a comfort. I dined last night at the Slowmores'; the night before at the Van Sluypperkins'. The Slowmores' chef got up their dinner. Of course it was gorgeous, but *heavy!* 'Well,' I remember thinking, in the middle of the fish, 'is it possible my immortal part is given me for such as this?' But the funny thing was that the Van Sluypperkins had had the same menu, the same flowers, the same wines. Everybody knows the Slowmores' income is fabulous. Why should the Van Sluypperkins try to live up to them, struggling with strange hirelings in the kitchen and dining room, who report the affair to the society column of the next day's newspaper, with their chief's name appended as having provided the dinner?"

"Why, indeed?" languidly responded Glenham, who liked little Mrs. Bob because she never bothered him to talk. Mrs. Bob sipped, like the birdling that she is, at the champagne-and-water in her *tazza* and resumed.

"What I was going to say is, that Talbot's old-fashioned ways (where else does one see such a grizzled negro butler take off the cloth and fetch fresh glasses for the after-dinner wines ?) convey to the minds of some of his guests a distinct assurance that he represents the class of old New Yorkers who can afford to be eccentric. The new people don't really admire it. They wouldn't attempt it in their own homes for a kingdom. They don't appreciate the ease, the mellow charm of Talbot's atmosphere."

"By Jove, they must appreciate his port," said Glenham, surveying the topaz sparkle of the liquid in his glass, with cordial approbation. "There's color for you, Mrs. Stryker! It is like my collie's eyes. No; it is like the eyes of the young lady who sits near Talbot, with the bunch of yellow roses in her yellow gown. I dare not mention names, for I see she thinks we are discussing her."

"*That* girl!" said Mrs. Bob, with fearless unconcern. "She may have great, big, languishing, yellow eyes, but I can't endure her. For a debby who came out only last November, Maud Grafton is the most self-possessed and determined young person of my acquaintance. Mark my words, Mr. Glenham, if Mr. Talbot sees much more of her, he's gone."

"Suppose I take him somewhere for a cruise," said Glenham, looking a little alarmed, for Talbot was the one chosen of his soul among all other men to be his comrade.

"It wouldn't be the first time the experiment was tried," said Mrs. Bob mischievously. She remembered the occasion, two years back, when Glenham had fairly turned tail and sailed around the globe, to avoid a dangerous crisis of the kind. "Well, I advise prompt action. He may have no idea that he's in danger. For a man of the world, our friend has a most unworldly soul ; and it's no business of mine. Life is too complicated, as we live, to go to mixing in other people's love affairs. But not only is that girl what, in Baltimore, we'd call an outrageous flirt, but she's cold as a stone inside—calculating, and quietly determined to improve her condition by getting out of her family groove before another season's over. Yes, she knows we are talking about her, but I don't care a snap. She poses to Talbot as an adorer, of the silent, speechless type. By the way, Mr. Glenham, you know everything; why did Talbot never' marry ?"

"Good Heavens ! my dear madam, you are like an electric shock!" exclaimed Glenham. At this moment there was an inter-

ruption.   Talbot had just leaned forward to
take a glass of wine with Mrs. Malbone, pre-
paratory to the general reaching down after
dropped gloves and fans that heralds
feminine departure from the table.   A lull
followed the merry chatter of the group.
The large room was brimming with im-
prisoned warmth and light and comfort.
On the rich crimson of the plush hangings
the high lights glanced like the glow from
rubies.   The air was heavy with the scent of
lilacs and roses, heaped, in massive wine-
coolers of beaten silver, upon the shining
board.   In the half-silence thus falling on
the company they heard the burst of a
wintry storm upon the windows, and above
its bluster, hoarsely tremulous but distinct, a
woman's voice was singing in the street :

> No more to chiefs and ladies bright
> The harp of Tara swells.

"Goodness, what a gruesome sound!"
said little Mrs. Bob, shivering.   She saw

Glenham glance at Talbot, and her eyes followed his. Their host had certainly grown paler, the glass trembled in his hand. With a sign he summoned the butler, who immediately left the room.

"Mr. Talbot is ill, I fear," whispered Mrs. Malbone's neighbor in her ear, and that lady, slowly taking the hint, arose, and gathering dames and damsels in her wake, departed up the stairs. From the servants, who followed them with coffee, the ladies reassured themselves as to Talbot's health, Maud Grafton, in particular, with a somewhat proprietary air, taking the lead in inquiry. Ascertaining that their host was much as usual, Mrs. Malbone subsided into a broad armchair with her satellite, Mrs. Carver, at her elbow; and Mrs. Bob, after toasting herself thoroughly before a huge wood fire, picked out a corner of a sofa, where, with cushions all about her, she soon became the center of a group of women

15

who one and all voted her "a perfect
dear, too sweet for anything," the acme
of feminine eulogium.

All, indeed, but Maud Grafton. This
young woman, who, until now, had enlisted
under Mrs. Bob's banner with meekness, if
inwardly remonstrant, chose now to sit aloof,
radiant in the wide circle of light cast by
the shade of a standing lamp. She had a
portfolio of etchings in her lap, and her pale
cheeks were flushed with some inward excitement. Once, when Mrs. Stryker happened to catch her eye, the astute little
lady read there a defiance that fairly startled
her.

"It's worse even than I thought," murmured the older of the duelists. "But, oh!
the pity of it!"

They were sitting, by common consent, in
the library, the great drawing rooms with
their pier-glasses, groups of statuary, and
crystal chandeliers, having, in their formal

chill, no charm for women to compare with that of a genuine "man's room," lived in and warm to the core with past good-fellowship. The re-entrance of the gentlemen was always preluded at Talbot's house by a tea-table, carried in by the ancient butler, and set at the elbow of the guest of honor among the ladies. On this occasion, Mrs. Malbone, who was much too grand to make tea, besides being interested in a stolid way in the particulars of a divorce case Mrs. Carver was pouring into her ears, waved the man aside. Then Mrs. Bob, rising to the emergency, intercepted a movement on Miss Grafton's part, and beckoned the man to her own neighborhood. As her pretty white fingers, flashing with many gems, twinkled in and out among the ponderous tea-things from which Talbot's mother had been wont to serve the cheery beverage, Mrs. Bob laughed her merry, lawless laugh.

"Checkmate again, my young lady!" the

little woman said. " But I suppose your time will come !"

A reluctant prophesy, which seemed likely to be fulfilled, if one might judge from the manner of the master of the house. Flushed, animated beyond his wont, Talbot, on coming into the room, went at once toward Miss Grafton's side, entering into a conversation of so evidently personal a character that people looked at each other in astonishment. It was as if Talbot meant to take this method of letting his friends know the truth of what had been, till then, the merest floating gossip.

And now the party, breaking into groups of twos or threes, wandered about the rooms, handling Talbot's books, eying his porcelains and pictures—a collection notable for excellence in this dilettante age of New York art-history. In an alcove, framed by the projection of two bookcases, hung a portrait of Talbot's mother, pink-tinted,

smiling, with bunches of pale brown ring-
lets on either temple, a white gown and a
vaporous blue scarf. Below it stood an antique harp, of a pattern seen in American
homes at the beginning of this century, but
unfamiliar now. The gilding, although
dulled by time, was fine, and the decora-
tions of painted wreaths of sweet-pea were
remarkably well preserved. " Query ?" said
Langford to the young lady at his side.
" Is this a souvenir of the lady who watches
over it, or simply bric-a-brac ? "

"Oh! it must have been his mother's,"
said Miss Carroll carelessly, stretching out
her gloved hand to run it across the strings.
Tuneless, yet pathetic, was the answer of
the slumbering spirit within the instrument.
A sigh rather than a wail, an echo of a
heartbreak, was breathed upon the air.

Glenham, on duty with Mrs. Malbone,
had not been able to keep his honest, anxious eyes from roving in the direction of

Talbot's *tête-à-tête*. He had seen Miss
Grafton's lashes fall, her face, half-shaded
by a great feather fan, assume a look of virgin innocence. He had seen Talbot's eye
kindle with an eager fire, his whole air indi-
cating an almost boyish disregard of comment from lookers-on.

"Good God!" said Glenham to himself.
"It's the most barefaced infatuation I ever
saw. *That* man sacrificed to *that* girl, who
is not worthy to tie his shoes. Where was
I that matters got so far without my knowing it? He won't speak here—if he hasn't
spoken—but there's the rub ; *has* he spoken,
or is there yet a chance?"

The twang of the harpstrings answered
him. Talbot, as he had done once before
that evening, started, shuddering. He
gasped, passed his hand over his eyes, gave
a quick glance at the group around the harp,
rallied, and tried to take up the thread of
his conversation with Miss Grafton. But

with a difference. Glenham, drawing a
long, deep sigh of relief, met a mocking
glance from Mrs. Bob.

" Where did he get this dear, quaint old
instrument?" repeated Miss Carroll. " I
am sure it has a history."

" I'll tell you," said Mrs. Bob, looking
saucily at Talbot, who had risen, and with
his unwilling companion was coming toward
them, " for I've already asked. At a bric-a-
brac shop on Broadway. In our part of the
world we either inherit heirlooms or go
without them."

During the week following the dinner,
Glenham saw nothing of his friend, either at
their club or, according to their custom,
to be riding for hours daily in the park. At
the end of that time he went to Talbot's
house, finding him alone in the dining room
sitting over his wine, a couple of fox-terriers
in chairs on either side of him watching his

every movement while apparently subdued into attitudes of repose, with their noses touching their fore-paws.

"Ha! Glenham! This is a happy thought of yours," he said, dislodging a terrier to offer his friend a chair, the dog, nothing daunted, springing with prompt agility to nestle on his master's knee. Glenham saw on Talbot's face lines of care that in a man of his age come only too readily at the chafing of circumstances. He even fancied that Talbot had grown grayer in a week. The two men smoked for a while, in silence, as old comrades are privileged to do, and, after some desultory talk, Talbot spoke abruptly:

"What brutal weather we've been having; worthy of our New York March at her worst! I'm outdone with it, and shall start for Florida to-morrow."

"St. Augustine, and that sort of thing!" asked Glenham.

"Not if I know myself. The Indian

River now, and perhaps I'll wind up in the West Indies. I'd ask you to come along, old man, but I think you'd put a bullet through me for a bore, before two days were over."

"Well, I've tried your quality before," was Glenham's answer. He felt pretty sure that confidence would come, and come it did.

"Glenham," said his friend presently, in somber tones, "you saw what happened here the other night? I know, for I read it in your face."

"This is a bid for my congratulations," said Glenham hoarsely, his heart thumping with real pain.

"That depends on how you look at it. If you mean that I am going to marry Miss Grafton, set your mind at rest; I have not asked her; I shall not ask her; though I'll own I came precious near it. No, not her, nor anyone. When a man's possessed by by-gones to the extent I am, you may give him up. I'm a hopeless case, Glenham—a hopeless case."

He was silent for a while, the fox-terrier licking his hand first, then standing on its hind legs to rest its fore-paws on his waistcoat in the attempt to lick his face.

"You saw how the spirit in the old harp convicted me of folly? That and another incident have roused in my brain of late a witches' Sabbat of old memories. I long for the South—the South where I loved and suffered—where, as a lad of twenty, all the poetry of my life was written on one page, then sealed from sight till now. I have long had an idea—the most Quixotic sort, no doubt—that I might hunt up Lénore Detreville and her children, and do something to help them in their strait. I heard of her, you know, after I came on her harp in the hands of a Broadway dealer, and recognized it by the initials on the plate. I traced her to a country neighborhood in Carolina, where she was living, a widow with two children, in the poorest kind of way. That was two years ago, and when I heard she had moved away leaving no clew that I could follow, I made up my mind that chapter of my life was done and forever put away. But it isn't, Glenham. I'm not that sort. Confound me, I wish I were. In the midst of our dinner, the other night, the sound of a street-singer's voice, chanting the old tune Lénore used to sing for me on summer nights in the Rose Hill drawing room, went through me like a knife. In a moment I seemed to smell the Cape jasmines in the garden outside, and to see the big stars shining in the Southern sky. My heart swelled with the wish to love, and to be loved as I was then. The passionate delight in Lénore's touch and presence seemed to tingle in my veins. Was it any wonder that I acted like a madman?"

"It is impossible that you shouldn't find Mrs.—er—Haskett again, if you set about it in good earnest," said Glenham, in his practical way. "But I'll warn you, Talbot, you're no fit subject for that sort of experiment. You have dwelt upon this thing for so long now, it is like a monomania. If you did meet her, no doubt it would be more trying than anything that has past. Pshaw! this is drivel between you and me. Hang it all, Talbot, why didn't you run away with Miss Detreville that time and be done with it? It would have been all forgiven and forgotten by her people when the war was over. What were those four years anyhow, in comparison with the twenty odd that have elapsed since you and I were boys."

"Run away," said Talbot, with a grim smile; "why, my dear boy, have you forgotten the spirit of those Southern girls at the outset of the war? They actually yearned to immolate themselves on the altar of their country. When Lénore heard me say that I should feel it my duty to fight with the North, she cast me from her as old fanatics cut their offending hands off. After I *did* fight against her people, I knew I might as well try to get a river to run backward as to go after her again. Besides, you forget; she married her cousin, Major Haskett. We killed him in '65, and her father died a pauper from the war."

Without, the wind raved, and a dash of sleet smote on the windowpanes. Glenham, getting up, drew aside the curtain and looked out into the night. Shivering, he came back to his comfortable corner.

"Another storm," he said, "a night for wanderers to be abed, and yet I fancied I saw a tall woman across the street, bending before the blast and snow like a reed. Ah! what is that?"

Not a cry of distress, as they both fancied, but, as before, a woman's voice, singing the sad old song:

> No more to chiefs and ladies bright
>   The harp of Tara swells,
> The chord alone that breaks at night
>   Its tale of ruin tells.

"If not bewitched, what am I?" exclaimed Talbot, springing to his feet, his face twitching. "By Jove, Glenham, I can't stand this; I could swear that is Lénore Detreville's voice! Ring the bell, will you? No, stay! I'll go myself. I'll pay this singing woman any money never to come back here."

Glenham, whom curiosity led to lift the shade and look outside, saw Talbot's powerful form dart out into the storm and approach the hooded creature who stood clinging to the railing of the steps. In the white glare of the electric light, he saw, also, to his unqualified astonishment, the woman stretch out her arms toward his friend, then throwing them above her head with a gesture of despair, sway forward as if about to fall.

They bore her gently into the house. Talbot's old housekeeper took the fainting wanderer in charge, and Talbot told his friend that he had thus met again the love of his long-gone youth. When consciousness returned she plead pitifully to be taken to her child—her dying son—for whose necessity the gently born and nurtured woman, starving and friendless in the streets of the great city, had stooped to this cruelest extremity of effort. Lénore had recognized Talbot, who at first still believed himself to be the victim of hallucination when he identified her.

She had gone to his house, not knowing whose it might be, simply because there, a

week before, on the occasion of her first
direful attempt, generous alms had been
given her; money that till now had sufficed
to keep her and her sufferer in life.

Reunited to her boy for whose sake she
had braved and borne so much, believing
that employment and success would ulti-
mately come to him in the metropolis, Lénore almost forgot Talbot in her ecstacy of
hope that she might win back to health and
strength again the child who was more to
her sad heart than any lover.

Talbot suspected this, suspected it with a
pang, when, the crisis of her son's illness past,
he again met his old love face to face. She
had changed less than had at first appeared.
Her old willowy grace remained, her glorious
dark eyes shone out of a pale, moonlit face,
her occasional smile charmed him with a
reminiscence of past joys. The attitude
into which fate had thus forced her, of a sup-

pliant for his alms, filled him with reverential
tenderness. To gather her and hers into a
home was henceforth his dearest wish. How
to effect it, was the problem that puzzled
him day and night. Glenham came away
from the interview with Mrs. Haskett, in
which he acted for his friend trying to
phrase the offer of substantial help from Talbot, feeling profoundly sad and touched.
He had seen enough of the terrible after-
chapters of the war to know that Lénore's
was no unprecedented case. His chivalry
laid itself at the feet of this beautiful woman,
born to bestow, not ask for bounty, who was
now only a poor waif of the great Southern
wreck, beaten by wind and wave into an
alien port—a woman who wore her sorrows
like a crown. But more than all was he sad
because he saw what his friend was slower
in discerning—that Talbot could no more
rekindle the flame of love in her heart than
he could relight a lamp that had no oil.

16

Glenham trusted rightly in the healthy tone of Talbot's mind for adjusting the confusion that had so long possessed it. Lénore's presence in the flesh, his frequent talks with her, gradually weaned him from dwelling on illusions. His old self, that had so long walked like a ghost in the haunts of memory, died with a final throb. He was no more the fond young lover masquerading under the early snows that drop on the head of " forty year." He was a man, mature and generous, strong to rule himself and to think for others. His first care had been to secure for Lénore and for her son some trifling employment that robbed the situation of its sting; for he had insisted on establishing them in rooms looking on a city park, where she might watch the unfolding of the spring. Then he eased her sorest anxiety by promising to charge himself with the future of her son, her other child, a daughter, having been left to share the poverty of relatives in the South. In time Talbot hoped to bring the little family together, but of that she would not hear as yet.

Glenham's visits to Mrs. Haskett's new quarters were almost as frequent as those of Talbot. From the two she enjoyed a hundred marks of delicate sympathy. Nothing, however, went so promptly to her heart, melting her to exquisite tenderness, as when her old harp, restrung, found its way to her little sitting room. Sometimes she would run her thin fingers over it, but never again was heard in song the voice that had once caused Talbot's soul to "float like an enchanted boat upon the silver waves of her sweet singing."

Before the spring was fairly changed to summer, it became apparent that all plans for Lénore's future were to be interrupted by the strong hand that overreaches man's best reckonings. A cold, induced by exposure, passed into a malady her enfeebled frame could not resist.

In the first stage of her illness, Talbot found her restless, nervous, unlike the brave and self-contained woman she had shown herself to be.

"I have taken a liberty," he said, striving to speak lightly, although a chill of dread passed into his veins; "in spite of your refusal to let me send to fetch your daughter, I have arranged for her to come North with some friends returning this week to town. If all goes well, she should be with you by Saturday at latest."

Lénore's eyes shone brilliantly, a deep red spot flamed in either cheek. Ill as she was, she looked the embodiment of joy.

"She will come! I shall see her once again! My darling, my treasure, for whom I have been longing hour by hour ever since I left her in that sordid home. Now you have put the finishing touch to all your kindness."

"There is no need of words between us two," said Talbot. "The idea of that poor child needing you as you have needed her, has been haunting me. It is an actual relief to me to send for her. And the people with whom she will travel northward are all that you could wish—refined, whole-souled, kindly. The Carltons have no young people of their own, and will no doubt take her to their hearts."

"Thank God!" she said. "Oh! Lénore will be to her brother what I have been. Louis can support her until she finds work to do. Lénore must succeed—she is so clever—she is so noble—she has borne everything so bravely. Ah! all I had left to wish for was that you might know Lénore!"

A few nights later, after a struggle short and sharp, her watchers saw peace return to

her troubled brow.   She had heard a foot-
step on the stair.

The door opened and a girl, pale with anguish, but in Talbot's eyes a rare, fine image
of his Lénore at seventeen, swiftly crossed
the floor, throwing herself in an agony of
grief upon her knees beside the bed.

Talbot went to the window of the adjoining room and gazed out into the night.
Clouds were hurrying across the sky, fitful
and fantastic, as if to bear the tidings that a
soul was free.   He wondered if his heart too
were dead, that it had ceased to ache.   Then
the clouds passed, and the moon rode out
between them in unstained majesty.   From
the chamber that had held Lénore her son
came to him weeping.

"You are mine, now," Talbot said, holding his hand out to the handsome lad.   Only
to utter the words sent a quick thrill of
human warmth into him.

"But poor Lénore?" Louis said, faltering.

"Oh, she is mine, too," Talbot answered, trying to speak cheerfully, and again the door opened, and looking up, he saw his lost love's eyes shining upon him through her daughter's tears.

When it was noised abroad that the lad Talbot had adopted was the child of an early friend left destitute by war, many were the comments of society upon his action.

"Take my word for it," said Mrs. Bob, in her stall at a bazaar where, jauntily attired as a Russian peasant, she was vending Russian tea, "it's all very well about the boy, but for a girl as pretty as that one Mrs. Carlton has taken into her home, this fatherly enthusiasm will soon wear itself out. Talbot will find another place for her in that great big heart of his; at least, I hope so. I, for one, have no patience with martyrs."

"Talbot's no martyr," said Glenham, to whom the outspoken lady had addressed herself. "He is more cheerful, more equable than he has been in years. As for Miss Haskett, she's simply enchanting. If Talbot will give me leave, I shall propose for her myself."

"Don't, please," said Mrs. Bob, putting a slice of lemon in his glass: "that would leave the coast clear for our common enemy, Miss Grafton."

"*Haven't* you heard?" asked Glenham, in astonishment. "You, the headquarters of all gossip that is worth listening to? Her engagement to old Slowmore is announced, and before the year is out the enterprising Maud will be in possession of his abundant shekels."

"Goodness!" said Mrs. Bob.

A SUIT DECIDED.

A POPULAR writer for the *Cosmos Maga-zine* of New York, having accomplished an article about the home and haunts of old Gilbert White of Selbourne, the *Cosmos* editors, in whose eyes the article found favor, had instructed one of their wandering artists, then in London, to go down to Sel-bourne and make sketches of the house and grounds and church.

Robert Kenyon, the young man to whose lot fell this pleasant pilgrimage, left his lodging in town one August morning and, casting a light portmanteau and still lighter knapsack, with his staff and umbrella, into the hansom at his door, gave the driver orders to proceed to Waterloo station.

Kenyon had no very clear idea of the place of his destination. He vaguely recalled Gilbert White as an amiable old parson who wrote about birds and weather, and set down the dates of the annual appearance of all things that flew and grew and blossomed in his neighborhood.

The artist had put into his knapsack a roll of typed MS. sent to him by the editors, representing the impression made by Selbourne upon the author he was to illustrate; and this he meant, upon the first convenient opportunity, to consult. But mankind is apt to put off reading typed MS. It is a shade less interesting than MS. in pen and ink, and one must be born with a love for that.

Kenyon, even in the short run to Dorking, where he desired to tarry on the way, found metal more attractive for his eyes than the clever American lady's views of the abode of Gilbert White. He dawdled

at Dorking for a day or so, and after an
enfeebling interview with Bradshaw and
local railway guides, shipped his portmanteau by train to Guildford, and started
south on foot. His delight was in solitary
tramps, and, ere long, within thirty miles of
the huge heart of England, he struck into
a region of rolling hills abloom with purple
heather, and came out upon a summit where
a stone tower marks the highest point of
the North Downs.

It was a clear morning, and after buy-
ing for a penny permission from an old
woman to mount the tower, he faced
one of the most glorious views in England. Five counties clad in midsummer
garb lay at his feet, and all about him
were broken hills and deep hollows filled
with heath and furze and bracken or cluster-
ing woods.

As Kenyon, descending from the tower,
climbed up over the door outside, to study

a half-effaced inscription in Latin, placed there by an Evelyn, descendant of the gossiping old chronicler of the court of Charles II., and forbear of the present lord of the neighboring manor, he heard a voice of a kind often breaking the repose that hangs around Old-World shrines—a voice not mellowed by soft English airs, but sharpened by the dry winds of the Western Continent.

"It's a fine open piece of country, and salubrious, no doubt," observed a gentleman wearing a high hat set back upon his crown, and what in America is known as a "business suit" of tweeds, wrinkled and baggy at the knees. "But I can't say I perceive any remarkable points about this landscape, except the Crystal Palace, that I'd as lief forget since the day you brought my lumbago back walking me over it. However, I guess it'll even up on historical association. They generally do. So, come on, Idalia, trot out your history, and let's get it over while I've got strength to listen."

"Sh—sh! papa!" said a girl's reproving tones; and at once the obedient gentleman, with a glance at Kenyon and a shrug of comical resignation to authority, was silenced.

Kenyon, coming back to *terra firma*, ventured a look at the historical Idalia, whom he found to be a young and very pretty girl, attired in the soft blending of grays and white seen in the plumage of a gull, and carrying a notebook and pencil in her hand. Piqued, apparently, by the unconsciously approving survey bestowed on her by the stranger, she went off to ascend the tower, at which the gentleman in tweeds relaxed his decorum and sidled up in Kenyon's immediate vicinity.

"Pleased to meet you, sir," he said cordially. "My name's McCunn—Cyrus K. McCunn, of Sago Falls, Wisconsin, now a resident of New York City. I am traveling with m' wife and daughter, an' m' wife, who's rather fleshy, draws the line at towers, and summits generally; but I have yet to see any eminence in art or nature that can daunt the spirit or take the wind out of Miss McCunn."

"You are fortunate in your companion," said Kenyon, in a perfunctory way.

"Yes, sir, very," said the good-natured Mr. McCunn. " But to tell you the facts of the case, it was all very well on our last two visits to Europe, when we kept on the beaten tracks and did the regular things set down on the guidebooks, that you can read up at night for the next day, and check off when you've finished them. I flatter my-self I stood that like a man. But it's Miss McCunn's last caper that her mother and I feel like speaking up against, only, of course, we don't. This trip, she's taken it into her head to include the by-ways and less familiar

places that have to do with a course of literature she and some other ladies went in for,
last Lent, in New York City. I believe
Miss McCunn's to read a paper before the
class, next Lent," he added, with a twinkle
in his eye.

"Good! Perhaps here's my chance to hear
about Gilbert White," came into Kenyon's
mind. But he suppressed satiric comment,
and Mr. McCunn again took up his tale.

"Just now, it's Southern England and
the cathedral towns, we're after chiefly,
I believe. Miss McCunn's paper's to be
about the town she likes the best. I hope
it'll be a short one. Winchester, where we go
next, has a good-sized cathedral and schools
and almshouses, too, I'm told, and would
take longer than the others to do, archæolog-
ically, as Miss McCunn means to do it. I
hope she won't take much of a fancy to
Winchester. There must be some of 'em
shorter. If her mother and I could only

sit in hotels, or even in carriages and
wait for her.   But m' wife says it isn't the
thing to let a young lady go around alone
in the old countries, though England isn't
as bad as it was on the Continent of Europe.
Yes, sir, I've known myself in by-gone days
to pity the sorrows of the unfortunate hack-
men, but, by George, it isn't a patch on the
waiting I've done for Miss McCunn.   I suppose we've got to take the consequences of
her having graduated No. 1 at the Skowhegan
Female College, in our State, when she was
sixteen, three years ago.   And since we
moved to New York to live, it's been nothing but masters and lectures and subscribing
to magazines and libraries.   We take six
American, three English, two French, and
one German periodical, sir.   Miss McCunn
cuts the leaves of all of 'em, and puts marks
in the articles she thinks best for her mother
and me to read.   But to tell you the truth,
sir, by the time I've looked at the advertise-

ments, front and back, I'm pretty apt to drop asleep, of an evening, over most of 'em."

Kenyon, basely conscious of fellow-feeling, here broke into a cheery laugh; and at this juncture the young lady, who had been jotting entries in her little book, rejoined them.

"I think I have all I need now, papa," she said, in a businesslike way. "And if you would like to return to the carriage to mamma and go on to Wootton, I'm ready."

"All right, Idalia," responded her father, preparing to move on, in a stiff fashion that suggested to Kenyon the first locomotion of a cab-horse after a wait. "Have you found out yet who's the owner of this eminence and tower?"

"Oh! yes, the lord of the manor, of course. 'Gulielmus Johannes Evelyn, Dominus Manorii,' the old one was called."

"Did he put all that on his visiting card,
17

I wonder?" said Mr. McCunn. "Well, sir, I'll bid you good-morning. I'd like to make you acquainted with my daughter, Miss McCunn, Mr. ——"

"Kenyon," supplied the young man, taking off his hat to the girl, who bowed and blushed slightly. "And a countryman of your own, Mr. McCunn."

"My dear sir, allow me to shake hands with you," said the other warmly. "I beg your pardon a thousand times, but I took you for a Britisher."

Kenyon laughed again, as he parted with them, and smiled more than once at the recollection of the prize pupil of Skowhegan Female College and her resigned parent. And more than once, also, he caught himself reverting admiringly to the prize pupil's erect figure, her peach-blossom cheeks, and her thick masses of waving golden hair.

Striking north by compass over the cattle-tracked common, he at last found his be-

lated way to the public at Wootton Hatch,
where, under the portraits of the queen and
sundry Evelyns, he dispatched a lunch of
bread and cheese and beer ; then, resuming
his line of march, went on through seven
miles of lovely rural landscape to Guildford,
where he took train for Alton, the station
nearest Selbourne.

Now, indeed, there was no longer time to
delay informing himself about the object of
his jaunt, and taking out the MS. Mr. Kenyon speedily ran over its contents. The
author, it should be said, was none other
than the accomplished Mrs. Euretta Hardy
Lodge, whose sketches of foreign travel are
so favorably known throughout her native
country, and whose charming " Glimpses at
Avon" Kenyon had illustrated the year before for another magazine; and as he
read on to the end, he felt she had, here, ac-
quitted herself well. He remembered all,
now—the very look of the copy of " White's

Selbourne," with its engravings of birds and beasts and insects, over which he used as a little boy to pore in his uncle's old rectory in the New England town where he grew up! And then the train slowed beside a platform, and " Alton " was written on a sign before his eyes.

Taking a rusty little trap, Kenyon, who had had, for the day, enough of tramping, drove through a region beautiful as many-shaded verdure and lengthening shadows of the afternoon could make it. But owing to the extraordinary depth of the lanes, " worn" (*vide* G. White himself) "by the traffic of ages, and the fretting of water down through the first stratum of freestone, and partly through the second, in many places sixteen or eighteen feet beneath the level of the fields," there was little scenery until the great chalk-hill above the village came into sight.

The cart climbed up the single narrow

street and deposited our artist at the "Queen's Arms," and Kenyon bethought him, as it was then well on to seven o'clock, to order dinner.

"What can I have?" he asked of the landlady.

"Chops, sir, or bacon an' heggs, or whatever you please to choose, sir, if you can wait. But there's a joint down for the hother party, sir, hand a pair of fowls—hand hit's hordered hat seven o'clock, sir, hin the sitting room, hupstairs."

"Very well," said Kenyon, seeing what was expected of him. "Then I'll take my share of the joint at seven—and soup, I suppose, and a tart to follow. I only hope the other party'll be on time."

"Who beside myself has chanced to wander to this sweet and placid nook?" he wondered, strolling out presently for a glimpse at the little church.

The church door was unlocked, and he

heard people talking within. Going to the portal, he ventured a glance inside and beheld, in custody of the witch-like old woman carrying the keys, a pair in whom he recognized the acquiescent McCunn and Skowhegan's pride, Idalia! On a tombstone without sat a large lady fanning herself with a palm-leaf fan, who smiled on him blandly in response to his salutation.

"I'm right afraid of these churches," she volunteered to say. "They 'most always give me a check of perspiration. I think this is the eighteenth or nineteenth sacred building my daughter and husband have done this summer. Daughter never tires of churches, now. But then, she never gets tired of anything. Often and often I say to her, 'Daughter, stretch yourself out for a half hour every day on the recliner, now, and it'll add ten years to your life.'"

"I had the pleasure of making acquaintance with Mr. and Miss McCunn at

Leith Hill, this morning, madam," said Kenyon. " But I had no idea I should so soon meet them again, and in this rather unusual place."

" Oh ! nothing's too unusual for daughter !" answered the lady in a monotonous voice, with an unchanging countenance. Kenyon, accepting this as final, bowed again and betook himself to a study of the old yew tree, coeval with the church, which, measuring in White's day three-and-twenty feet in girth, has now expanded to an actual circumference of twenty-seven, and a reputed one of thirty-six feet.

Here he was joined by Mr. McCunn, who gave him cordial greeting.

" Mr. Kenyon, sir ! I'm delighted to meet you again. Of course you are stopping at the Queen's Arms, and I hope you will dine with us—unless," with a falling face, " you are the guest of the family at the house."

" I'm the veriest wayfarer, and, until to-
day, had no idea of what I was coming to.
I'm afraid our good hostess at the inn had
already made up her mind to billet me upon
the dinner ordered for you.   I fancy there
is no great run of custom in these parts.
But it's very kind to make me one of your
party, and I accept with thanks."

" Talk about Robinson Crusoe looking
for the tracks of a white man, sir," said
McCunn, walking beside him, following the
ladies, a moment later ; " and you can
understand my feelings when I meet a
fellow-citizen in a place like this.   I believe
I didn't mention to you this morning, that
the lady—an elegant lady, sir, an ornament
to American womanhood—who conducts
the literature class to which Miss McCunn
belongs, has written an article about this
venerable village that's to be published in
one of our leading magazines—no doubt
sir, you have heard of her—all Ameri-

cans are proud of Mrs. Euretta Hardy Lodge.

"And that is what brought *you* here?" Kenyon began, and refrained from finishing.

"Exactly," answered Mr. McCunn, appreciating Kenyon's point. "I remarked to you this morning that Miss McCunn's layout, at present, is the unhackneyed past. But I am pleased to say that she has given her mother and me reason to believe she will finish Selbourne in time for the 2:15 train from Alton to Winchester to-morrow. In the meantime, I have no great hopes of the bill of fare, have you?"

Their dinner, served in a stuffy sitting room by the light of a dimly burning oil lamp, was an experience happily brought soon to an end; and after it Kenyon strolled away with his cigarette, to enjoy the long soft evening light from the beech wood called "The Hanger," clothing part of the chalk cliff that dominates the village.

Stretching himself at length under a tree, he gazed down at the humble dwellings, the church, and " The Wakes " amid its ample lawns, all a hundred feet below ; and a reverie that was sweet and restful as England's atmosphere could make it, took possession of his soul.

" I *beg* your pardon," said, in rather distressful cadence, the voice of Miss McCunn ; " I *hate* to disturb you, but I'm quite sure I left my notebook there, when I climbed farther up the hill."

" So you did," remarked Kenyon, stirring himself to discover something square and hard under his left shoulder blade. " Why, what a fleet nymph you must be to have distanced me in getting here. I thought you had gone with your mother to her room."

" I came off when you and papa were waiting for your coffee," she said. " I did want to give my poor father a rest, and, besides, I like to be alone in an hour and place like this."

" That's an unkind hint," said Kenyon, getting upon his feet.

" Oh! please, I didn't mean to seem rude," she exclaimed. " I am going directly back to the inn."

" Don't go," he urged, admiring her girlish readiness to take alarm. " Sit down here a few minutes, and enjoy this pearly atmosphere, the deepening of all those greens and the exquisite charmed slumber of the homes nestled in leafage below—one never has such an impression of peace in any American landscape where man has settled."

The frank Idalia, bestowing on him a pleased smile, took her seat beside him on the cliff, and they began a talk that lasted until growing dusk sent her springing lightly as a young fawn down the hill-path, for a second time neglectful of the note-book, that compendium of valuable information, bound in green alligator-skin and edged and clasped with silver, that Kenyon again picked up and carried after her.

They met, walking in the middle of the village street, smoking a cigar, and wearing his hat a-tilt as usual, the unruffled Mr. McCunn.

" I cal'lated you young folks were off to-gether," he said pleasantly. " Idalia, my dear, your mother's about read up all the literature in that sitting room, I reckon ; and she's talking some of going to bed. Mr. Kenyon, sir, this place of resort aint as exciting as the Stock Exchange in New York City in a boom. Will you walk up and down a bit, and try one of my cigars? "

From his artless compatriot, our artist as-certained sundry details of his life and con-dition in the States. Cyrus K. McCunn, beginning life as a mechanic, had invented an automatic car-coupler, for use in railway trains, and, this proving a success, had for a number of years enjoyed an ample income from royalties paid by the companies which used it.

Having set out on the glittering road to wealth, the temptation of Cyrus had been next to add to his gains by speculation, and it was plain to Kenyon that the poor man's heart was left behind in the fevered atmosphere where dollars change hands before moth or rust has time to corrupt their sheen.

"If the ladies didn't mind my leaving them," he said pathetically, "you'd better believe, sir, that I'd be off from here at daybreak, and catch the next North German Lloyd's boat at Southampton sailing for New York. When they told me how near Winchester—that's our next stopping-place —is to Southampton, sir, I just thought of that steamer's gang-plank, and ached to be walking it—*ached*, Mr. Kenyon, ached! But m' wife has had nervous prostration,

and won't hear of being left; and Miss
McCunn—well, you can see what she is—as
nice and sweet a little girl as ever grew up—
and took such an education, that Mrs.
Euretta Hardy Lodge says it would be an
evidence of incomplete civilization not to
afford her *all* the advantages; and I s'pose
Mrs. Lodge is right. I never had any of
Miss McCunn's advantages myself; and m'
wife went to a country school, and don't
pretend to keep up with her. I guess we're
pretty plain people, Mr. Kenyon, sir, and it
would be natural to some girls who had Miss
McCunn's education and—if I say it, who
shouldn't—the money she has to spend, for
I don't count the dollars I shell out for her—
to hitch on to some of our stylish folks,
who'd be quick enough to take her up, and
travel about with her, or marry her off to a
count or lord. B'gosh, sir, I'd like to see
the lord that 'ud get Miss McCunn! My
girl had a bid to go to Europe this summer

with some of her high-flying friends, and what d'ye suppose she did? Why, sir, just came up and put her arms around my neck, and says, ' As long as I can coax my home-spun dad to travel, he's good enough for me!' Gee Whillikins, Mr. Kenyon, I'd 'a' traveled around creation with little Daly after that!"

Kenyon was up betimes, next day, stalking through dewy fields, starting the birds in the thickets, and the hares under his feet, to the Priory farm, where a civil farmer showed him the relics, still in process of ex-humation, of the old-time monastery once upon the spot, and, at parting, told the visitor that he had heard—a rare thing after midsummer—a nightingale's note the day before.

At ten o'clock, as early as he dared pre-sent himself at a private dwelling, Kenyon, who had come back to the village through sweet-scented lanes and tasseled hop-gar-

dens, offered his credentials at the house-
door of " The Wakes," to find himself most
kindly welcomed, and made free to sketch
such tokens of old Gilbert's life there as
might still be found.

When, at luncheon-time, he returned to
the inn, the McCunn family was seated
in a carriage at the door, about to drive
away.

" We shall keep a sharp eye on that article
of Mrs. Euretta Hardy Lodge's in the *Cosmos*, sir," said Cyrus, jumping down to shake
Kenyon elaborately by the hand. " I guess
Miss McCunn won't have to put a marker
in, to point *that* out to me."

" Miss McCunn will be putting the contents of her own notebook into print before
long, I fancy," said the young man, going
around to Idalia's side of the trap. " I hope,
by the way, you have that important volume
safe."

" I hope so, sir," answered the young

lady's father, in her stead. "For if she
didn't, I guess we'd all be making tracks
back to Selbourne to look for it, and I've
had enough of this antiquity in mine, thank
you, for some time to come. Now, Mr.
Kenyon, don't forget to hunt us up when
you get back to New York City. You'll
always find my name in the Directory, even
if I fail in business and have to move out
o' No. 4001 Fifth Avenue, where we hang
out now."

"I don't think that's likely, Mr. McCunn,"
said his lady stolidly, and her husband
chuckled, as if the contingency were in truth
a remote one.

"Good-by," said Idalia, letting her eyes,
blue as forget-me-nots, rest fearlessly on
Kenyon's, as she put her little gloved hand
in his. "I have written down what you
said last night about the charm that lies
in repose. It is strange Mrs. Lodge never
thought of calling our attention to that, in

18

class.   And I am sure your pictures will be beautiful."

"May I send you a little sketch of the church to your banker's care in London?" he asked. "I should be so glad to have you remember me by it."

"That's a handsome offer, sir," said Mr. McCunn, shaking hands again. "And Miss McCunn is glad to accept of it. Anything sent to the care of Messrs. Clayton, Jones & Co., London, will reach us till September 25th—and after that, please the Fates, we'll be on the briny, making the best time we can across the Western ocean."

Kenyon in due time forwarded the drawing, received in return for it a rather prim and sedately worded note on Irish linen paper, with a silver monogram, and—Idalia faded from his mind.

More than two years later, after he had sketched in Venice and Madrid and Vienna, had tried his luck in Russia and Constantinople, Kenyon dropped in one day in January upon his friend the editor of the *Cosmos Magazine* in New York. As they two, in connection with the Art Editor, finished the discussion of a series of drawings proposed for the coming year of the magazine, and Kenyon went into the outer office, he saw, waiting there under guard of the angels with typewriters who keep the editorial doors, a figure seated upon a chair. It was a woman, young and graceful, in mourning dress, holding in her hand a flat package that betokened MSS., left studiously unrolled. Through her veil of black net, he recognized the face, and strove to recall the name that ought to go with it.

"Why, Mr. Kenyon," she said, holding out her hand, and at once, he knew Idalia Mc—— "Now, what in the dickens is the rest of it?" he inquired of his inner man.

"My father will be *so* glad to hear of you again," she went on rapidly. "He took

such a fancy to you, you can't think.   And
if you *could* find time to visit us——"

"Nothing would give me greater pleasure," he said suavely, still harping eternally
on the string. " Mc——   What in the world
is she—I can't call her Miss McWhat?"

"I have a card here, and he is always at
home in the evening—since my mother's
death—and—other changes.   Now, I must
hurry, as I have an appointment with the
editor."

"You are by this time a full-fledged author?" Kenyon went on, as the recollection
of her notebook came back to him.

"They have printed two or three things
for me, here," she said, blushing. " But not
over my own name.   I took a fancy, when I
first wrote, to call myself—and the story
was liked so I was advised not to change
it—by a rather stupid little name—Olive
White."

"What, you are Olive White?"

"And I chose the last part of it because I remembered that dear little place, and a talk I had with you that influenced me so much. Good-by, and you'll come, won't you? I ask because it would so cheer my father up."

"Olive White is 'Miss Idalia McCunn,'" he repeated, reading the card she had left with him. "Why, I read that last story of hers when I was flat on my back in a sunny corner of Spain, and cried over it too, by Jove! What a queer thing for such grace and poetic fancy to have sprung from that parent stock. I must find time to look in on them some day."

If all the promises we mortals make to call upon chance encountered friends, were registered in heaven to our debit, it would be a serious addition to our stock of things to be atoned for. Robert Kenyon fully meant to visit the McCunns, but somehow he failed to do so, until the May number of the *Cosmos*, containing an especially charming little story from " Olive White," jogged his delinquent memory.

" I'll go this evening and take my chance," he said, decisively, and proceeded to hunt up Miss McCunn's address.

On finding the long-lost card, to Kenyon's surprise, their abode was recorded as not in Fifth Avenue, but in a remote eastern quarter of a side street, certainly one not to be selected by plutocracy for its dwellingplace. This fact served to whet Kenyon's appetite for search, and soon after dinner he made his way to the address indicated.

It was a poor house in a plain neighborhood, and the room, in which a maid-servant bade him wait, confirmed his astonishment at the change in the fortune of the McCunns. Was it possible that the father of Idalia had deceived him as to his circumstances? Where then was McCunn's successful car-coupler? Why had its profits

not continued to pour gold into the purse
of Cyrus K.?

"I call this neighborly," said a wan,
shabby, and grizzled edition of the Cyrus of
nearly three years back, who at that moment came into the little gas-lighted room.
"Mr. Kenyon, sir, I'm about as pleased to
see you, as if the U. S. Supreme Court had
pronounced a judgment in my favor. I told
Miss McCunn I was pretty sure the frowns
of Fortune upon our lot would make no
difference to you. I rather guess she felt
kind of badly at meeting you, remembering
how different things had been before—that
is to say, she felt badly when you didn't
call. But I told her a traveler like you—a
man that travels for the love of it, and can't
get his fill of those old antiquities—had
gone off somewhere to Japan, or to the
South Pole, and would drop in when he got
back."

"I'm here, as you see, Mr. McCunn," said

Kenyon, touched by the man's insistent cheerfulness. "And I'm more sorry than I can say to hear that affairs have gone ill with you."

"It can't be helped now, Mr. Kenyon, and I've no call to whine over spilt milk, sir. But it 'most killed m' poor wife, and pneumonia did the rest. She never could be got to understand where the money went, and b'gosh, sir, few people did. With what funds I had, I dipped into a lot of things that went against me—and, while I was off in Europe that last time, a strong combine of capitalists, holding a patent infringing on my invention, ruined me ; but my case has gone to the Supreme Court, on appeal, sir, and I've still hopes—strong hopes— for Miss McCunn's sake, sir—for, though she don't know it, the doctor tells me I can't get over this trouble in my lungs. She works hard, does Miss McCunn, and you wouldn't believe the pleasure she takes in

settling bills out of her own little earnings.
She's become quite an authoress, you know,
sir. Tell you what, education's a mighty
fine thing, Mr. Kenyon. And how is art,
sir. Flourishing, I hope?"

" Pretty flourishing," said Kenyon; and
the entrance of Idalia struck him with a
strong sense of the girl's refined beauty in
her developed womanhood. He told her of
the pleasure he had had in her recent
stories, and she ran upstairs to fetch his
framed sketch of Selbourne Church, which
she took from her bedroom wall. The three
talked, and Kenyon lingered until eleven
o'clock warned him that his visit had lasted
long enough to make amerus for its delay
in beginning.

Kenyon went back, more than once, to
the little house in the unfashionable quarter. and when summer came found Idalia
making preparations for the transfer of her
invalid—whose malady had now advanced

beyond concealment--to a cheap little
boarding place on the Jersey coast.

At Nahant, where he was stopping later
in the season, he wrote to inquire for them,
and received, in answer, a pitifully cheerful
note, saying that although the air had not
done all they expected for her father's
health, Idalia felt his spirits were kept
up by hope for the favorable termination of
his law suit in the autumn.   Kenyon had to
suppress a strong impulse to go down and
see about these matters for himself.   His
lifelong habit of scoffing at weakness of the
sentimental order was not to be conquered
in a day ; and, besides, he had promised his
friend Clive to cruise with him during
August in his yacht.

Through one cause or another our artist
did not return to town until late in Oc-
tober ; and, dropping in that evening to
dine at the Club, he found awaiting him a
note in Idalia's hand informing him of her

father's serious illness, asking him to call, and dated some days back.

Summoning a cab, he drove immediately to the house, a blank feeling that all might be over having taken possession of his mind. A light, however, was burning in the invalid's room, and a message was brought him with the request to walk upstairs.

Poor Cyrus K. McCunn, with the look upon his face almost of death, lay on his pillows apparently in coma; on one side, a nurse held a glass with stimulant, and on the other knelt Idalia, clinging tearfully to his chill hand. She gave Kenyon a quick greeting and then resumed her study of her father's face, while the nurse glided around the bed and addressed the newcomer.

" He has been asking for you, sir, and it is possible he may rouse again; in which case you could answer the question that seems to weigh upon his mind. But there is no telling, and he may go off as he is."

The artist, who was a soft-hearted man, and little used to scenes of this kind, was at first painfully embarrassed and oppressed. The sight of the woe-stricken girl about to be left to fight her way, unaided, through the world, roused in him not only a desire to help her, but a tenderer feeling, that he had fancied overcome. Drawing nearer, he took her trembling hand in his ; and as she started and shivered, he noticed a hot blush settle upon her still averted face.

But he did not loose his hold, and soon the nurse looked up from her patient, to whom she had just administered the stimulant.

"Now, he is coming to," she whispered.

"Idalia, is Mr. Kenyon there?" were the next words to break the stillness of the room.

to do anything I can for you," said his visitor.

"Mr. Kenyon, sir, I was sure you'd not mind my sending. The world and I are about settling up accounts. A little while ago, sir, thinking of what might come, I made a new will—it's all straight, signed and sealed, in my lawyer's hands—and I've named you trustee of my entire estate, sir. No offense meant, Mr. Kenyon; but, if it bothers you, I want to ask your pardon, now. Sole trustee—Idalia knows what I—haven't strength to say. It's because—we believe in you, Mr. Kenyon—Miss McCunn and I."

"I accept the charge. You may trust your child to me, Mr. McCunn," said Kenyon, tightening his clasp upon the little hand. *That* much, he felt, was tangible, the rest he believed to be a mere delusion of a dying brain.

"Is that so, Mr. Kenyon?" the man said, a pleased look coming amid the violet shadows on his countenance. "Then I guess it's about the last thing to trouble me. She won't let the business bother you any more than she can help. It'll be a big lot of money to look out for, but she's a level-headed girl, and a good, dear, loving girl, that deserves every cent of it, and more. God bless my little one—why, Daly dear, who'd 'a' thought you'd be crying the day the news came I'd won my suit and you're one of the champion heiresses of America . . . Mr. Kenyon, sir, . . . to hear *to-day* that the Supreme Court . . . has decided . . . in my favor . . . is what I call a close connection!"

"Oh! father, father," cried Idalia imploringly, throwing herself on the bed in a fresh burst of grief, as Kenyon loosed her hand and started back. "Speak to me again—don't leave me alone like this."

But with his last grim effort at a joke, McCunn's voice had failed, and he lay quite deaf and still. Very soon they saw that he had passed beyond earthly jurisdiction to appear before the final Arbiter.

A deep red flush burned upon Kenyon's cheek, as with some constraint he bent over the weeping girl and whispered in her ear. Then with a sudden confiding movement, like a child eager for consolation from the one it loves, Idalia turned toward him and, with his arm about her, let him lead her from the room.

THE END.

www.ingramcontent.com/pod-product-compliance
Lightning Source LLC
Chambersburg PA
CBHW020512270326
41926CB00008B/841